T0026535

Invitation to Love

BY THE SAME AUTHOR

Open Mind, Open Heart
The Mystery of Christ
The Heart of the World
Awakenings
Reawakenings
Crisis of Faith, Crisis of Love
Intimacy with God
Daily Reader for Contemplative Living

Invitation to Love

Love

The Way of Christian Contemplation

20th Anniversary Edition

Thomas Keating

B L O O M S B U R Y

LONDON · NEW DELHI · NEW YORK · SYDNEY

First published in Great Britain 2011
Reprinted 2014

Copyright © St Benedict's Monastery, 1992, 2012

The moral right of the author has been asserted

No part of this book may be used or reproduced in any manner
whatsoever without written permission from the Publishers except in the case
of brief quotations embodied in critical articles or reviews. Every reasonable
effort has been made to trace copyright holders of material reproduced in this
book, but if any have been inadvertently overlooked the Publishers would be
glad to hear from them.

Bloomsbury Publishing Plc
50 Bedford Square
London WC1B 3DP

www.bloomsbury.com

Bloomsbury is a trademark of Bloomsbury Publishing Plc

Bloomsbury Publishing, London, New Delhi, New York and Sydney

A CIP record for this book is available from the British Library.

ISBN 978 1 4411 8757 4

10 9

Typeset by Newgen Imaging Systems Pvt Ltd, Chennai, India
Printed in the United States of America

Contents

Acknowledgments

This book is the fruit of not only my experience, but of Contemplative Outreach, Ltd., a network of faith communities seeking to recover and to assimilate the contemplative dimension of the gospel and to share it with others. The insights offered here have been refined by reflection, dialogue, and, above all, by the common experience of an increasing number of persons practicing since 1975. Thus, the book is an approximation of where we are now in our understanding of the Christian spiritual journey as a life process.

I must first of all thank the monastic community of St. Benedict's, Snowmass, Colorado, and especially its remarkable abbot, Father Joseph Boyle, OCSO, who have supported this work and welcomed the intensive retreats as one facet of their generous hospitality.

I thank the members of Chrysalis House, our lay contemplative community in Warwick, N.Y., who incarnated the vision of Contemplative Outreach in visible form for the eleven years of the service; the National Faculty of Contemplative Outreach, who share responsibility for developing resources and training presenters of Centering Prayer and intensive retreats; our National Board of Directors and Advisors over twenty-two years, especially its President, Gail Fitzpatrick Hopler; the Coordinators of some one hundred and twenty regions around this country and overseas, especially the Philippines, England, Central Africa, the Dominican Republic and South Africa; and the local support groups that meet together weekly and in regional or national conferences every year. This ever-widening network of persons dedicated to the spiritual journey in the Christian tradition is forming a vast reservoir of the lived experience of contemplative prayer and of its application to daily life.

My heartfelt gratitude goes to the persons who staff the intensive retreats held monthly at the guest facilities at the Snowmass monastery. Our staff enables retreatants to enter at once into an ongoing contemplative community whose practice is unstinting service. During these retreats the material in this book has been discussed and lived by many sincere retreatants, with our staff serving as examples and guides to its meaning and practice.

My special thanks go to Judith Clark who worked with me over a period of three years to arrange the basic ideas and various parts of this book. The final format I owe to Cynthia Bourgeault, without whose editing skills I could not have brought the manuscript to its final form. The devoted secretarial services of Patricia Johnson and Bonnie Shimizu have also made a substantial contribution.

Introduction

This book is the result of an ongoing effort to re-present the Christian spiritual path in a way that is accessible to contemporary followers of Christ. During the first sixteen centuries of the Church's history, contemplative prayer was the acknowledged goal of Christian spirituality for clergy and laity alike. After the Reformation this heritage, at least as a living tradition, was virtually lost. The recovery of the Christian contemplative tradition began in the twentieth century and it continues now, twenty years after the original publication of this book.

Throughout the early 1970s, a small group of Trappist monks at St. Joseph's Abbey, Spencer, Massachusetts, were reflecting on how they might contribute to this renewal. In 1975 the contemplative practice called Centering Prayer, based on the fourteenth-century classic *The Cloud of Unknowing*, was developed by Father William Meninger and offered at the guest house in Spencer to priest retreatants. A year later he made a series of audio tapes, which continues to be popular even to this day. The response to the method was so positive that introductory workshops were instituted on a regular basis and made available to everyone. Father Basil Pennington joined in this work and extended the introductory workshops to an ever-widening circle of places and persons.

In 1981, I resigned as abbot of St. Joseph's and moved to St. Benedict's Monastery, Snowmass, Colorado. The idea of a more intensive experience of Centering Prayer began to surface. In 1983, the first Intensive Centering Prayer Retreat was held at the Lama Foundation, San Cristobal, New Mexico. Since then, Intensives have been given at St. Benedict's Monastery and in other locations.

A number of weekly support groups grew up in various areas of the country, and the need to organize became evident. In 1984, Contemplative Outreach, Ltd. was established to coordinate efforts to introduce Centering Prayer to persons seeking a deeper life of prayer and to provide support systems and ongoing training opportunities capable of sustaining their commitment. Continuing practice also created the need for a more comprehensive conceptual background in order to understand the practice and to integrate its effects into daily life.

In the Christian tradition, contemplative prayer has never been a privatized spiritual experience in the service of "altered states of consciousness" or self-actualization. With the spiritual thirst awakened through encounter with God's presence during Centering Prayer periods, the need became more insistent for a representation of the classic Christian spiritual path in a way consistent with contemporary sciences, in particular, the insights of modern psychology.

It is my conviction that the language of psychology is an essential vehicle in our time to explain the healing of the unconscious effected during the dark nights which Saint John of the Cross describes. For one thing, it is a language that is better understood than the traditional language of spiritual theology, at least in the Western world. It also provides a more comprehensive understanding of the psychological dynamics which grace has to contend with in the healing and transforming process.

The first attempt toward providing a comprehensive frame of reference for the experience of contemplative prayer began as conferences at the two-week intensive retreat at Lama in 1983. These conferences were refined over the course of several years at other intensive workshop-retreats. In October 1986, these were filmed as a seventeen-part video cassette series called "The Spiritual Journey." Seven more parts were added. The series has become an important teaching tool, along with the resource book *Open Mind, Open Heart,* first published in 1986 and reissued in 2006, for ongoing support groups.

The present book is a selective development of material originally presented in those tapes. It is an attempt to provide a road map, as it were, for the journey that begins when Centering Prayer is seriously undertaken and to point to some of the recognizable landmarks on the journey, as well as to its ultimate destination. The latter is not so much a goal to be attained, as an ever more resolute commitment to the journey. This book also reflects the ongoing insights of many persons practicing Centering Prayer and sharing their experiences over many years.

Although this book seeks to establish a dialogue between the insights of contemporary psychology and the classic Christian spiritual masters, its primary goal is *practical*: to provide a solid conceptual background for the practice of contemplative prayer and the spiritual journey for our time. We are called to this journey not just for our own personal growth, but also for the sake of the whole human family.

As this book will show, one of the biggest impediments to spiritual growth is that we do not perceive our own hidden motivations. Our unconscious, prerational emotional programming from childhood and our overidentification with a specific group or groups are the sources from which our false self—our injured, compensatory sense of who we are—gradually emerges and stabilizes. The influence of the false self extends into every aspect and activity of our lives, either consciously or unconsciously.

Centering Prayer, and more particularly contemplative prayer for which it is a preparation and a first step, brings us face to face with this "false self" in several ways: The initial act of consent to letting go of our surface "I" with its programs, associations, commentaries, etc., in itself drives a fatal wedge into the false self. As we rest in prayer, we begin to discover that our identity is deeper than just the surface of our psychological awareness.

The regular practice of centering prayer initiates a healing process that might be called the "divine therapy." The level of deep rest accessed during the prayer periods loosens up the hard-pan around the emotional weeds stored in the unconscious, of which the body seems to be the warehouse. The psyche begins to evacuate spontaneously the undigested emotional material of a lifetime, opening up new space for self-knowledge, freedom of choice, and the discovery of the divine presence within. As a consequence, a growing trust in God, a bonding with the Divine Therapist, enables us to endure the process.

Thus, contemplative prayer to which Centering Prayer leads us is a practical and essential tool for confronting the heart of the Christian ascesis—namely, the struggle with our unconscious motivation—while at the same time establishing the climate and necessary dispositions for a deepening relationship with God and leading, if we persevere, to divine union.

Meanwhile, the same process of letting go (of thoughts, feelings, commentaries, etc.), first experienced during the prayer period, becomes the basis for a practice of consent that can be carried into all of life, enabling us more and more to live the values of the gospel.

This book is part of a trilogy that contains the principal aspects of the Intensive Centering Prayer Retreat. *Open Mind, Open Heart* deals with the practice of Centering Prayer as a preparation to realize the gift of contemplation. *Invitation to Love* offers the conceptual background for the practice and for the Christian contemplative journey in general. *The Mystery of Christ* is an attempt to integrate both the practice and the conceptual background into the celebration of the liturgical year and the immersion in the mystery of Christ. Together they are meant to provide a comprehensive program with which to respond to the invitation of the Spirit to follow Christ in our time.

1

The Emotional Programs for Happiness

Centering prayer addresses the human condition exactly where it is. This prayer heals the emotional wounds of a lifetime. It opens up the possibility of experiencing in this world the transformation into Christ to which the gospel invites us.

God wants to share with us even in this life the maximum amount of divine life that we can possibly contain. The call of the gospel, "Follow me," is addressed to every baptized person. We have within us in virtue of our baptism all the grace-given powers we need to follow Christ into the bosom of the Father. The attempt to do this—to reach more deeply toward the love of Christ within us and to manifest it more fully in the world—constitutes the heart of the spiritual journey.

The journey has been presented in Christian tradition as an ascent. Images of ladders and upward journeys abound. But for most of us who undertake the journey today, in our age when developmental psychology and a greater understanding of the unconscious is widespread, the journey might more properly be seen as a descent. The direction, at least initially, is toward a confrontation with our motivations and unconscious emotional programs and responses. Our spiritual journey does not start with a clean slate. We carry with us a prepackaged set of values and preconceived ideas which, unless confronted and redirected, will soon scuttle our journey, or else turn it into pharisaism, an occupational hazard for religious and spiritual people.

The developmental character of human life has become much better known in the last hundred years, and it has enormous implications for the spiritual journey. Our personal histories are computerized, so to speak, in the biocomputers of our brains and nervous systems. Our memory banks have on file everything that occurred from the womb to the present, especially memories with strong emotional charges. In the first years of life, there is no consciousness of a self, but there *are* needs and our emotional responses to them, all faithfully recorded in the biocomputers of our brains. Already these computers are developing emotional programs for happiness—happiness at this stage meaning the prompt fulfillment of our instinctual needs. By the time we come to the age of reason and develop full reflective self-consciousness around the age of twelve or thirteen, we have in place fully developed emotional programs for happiness based on the emotional judgments of the child—even the infant.

Of all newborn mammals none is more helpless than the human infant. Other species have all kinds of useful instincts, but the infant depends completely on the reception he or she receives from the parent(s); the best he can do is to cry loudly to make his needs known. The most crucial instinctual needs in the first year of life are survival and the sense of security. The infant enjoyed a marvelous environment in the womb where all his needs were taken care of and where he felt perfectly safe. The new environment can hardly compare with the wonderful environment of the womb. The first need of the infant is to bond with his mother. His entire world is the mother's face, smile, and the heartbeat that reminds him of the safe environment of the womb. The infant's whole concern is the prompt fulfillment of his needs, the chief of which, along with food, is affection. The baby needs to be held, kissed, and caressed. Being picked up frequently to nurse or to have his diapers changed reinforces the bonding process with the mother. The bonding force of the universe is love. We can hardly exaggerate the amount of affection that the infant needs in order to feel safe. This feeling of security enables the emotional life of the child to unfold in a healthy way.

Suppose an infant comes into the world in an environment that is not welcoming or where he experiences hesitation about his arrival. He will then have an emotional hesitation to accept the adventure of life because his most important need, the biological necessity for security, is not met.

In the second year of the child's life, a more varied repertory of emotions develops, and the child experiences need for pleasure, affection, and esteem. These are present, of course, earlier in life, but now the child is differentiating himself from the environment and is beginning to experience himself as a body distinct from the other creatures crawling around on the floor. The child needs more than ever the warmth of affection and acceptance of parents and family. Along with this development of a body-self, the child begins to want his own way, manifesting the instinctual needs for power and control.

Suppose that one of these instinctual needs, necessary for biological survival, is perceived by the child to be withheld, either through competition with other siblings or through exposure to an environment that is hazardous. Maybe he lives in a locale where the great tragedies of our time are taking place—guerrilla warfare, epidemics, destitution, starvation—where there is daily risk of losing one's parents, and where violence is the order of the day. In such situations it becomes more and more difficult for a child to consent emotionally to the goodness and beauty of life.

Again, the child may have a handicap that prevents him from taking part in games. Or, through sibling competition or a vague sense of unwantedness, he may come to feel inferior. In any case, the fragile emotional life of the child, if there are any negative influences, begins to develop compensatory needs to offset the frustration of its instinctual needs, or to repress painful memories into the unconscious. We may not remember the events of early childhood, but the emotions do. When events occur later in life that resemble those once felt to be harmful, dangerous, or rejecting, the same feelings surface. We may not be fully aware of where the force of those feelings is coming from.

Even with the most well-intentioned and capable of parents, we have to deal with the influences of the culture and peer groups. Although we may not have experienced serious traumas, all of us have experienced that emotional fragility of early childhood and hence bring with us some wounds as a result. Some have enormous wounds because of the misunderstanding or fumbling of parents or the lack of parents.

If a child is severely deprived of affection in infancy, especially during the first year or two, he has no way of discerning the cause. He has only feelings to go by. All he knows is that he is not being loved, and this deprivation may lead to deep-seated feelings of hostility or fear.

If we felt deprived of security, the particular security symbols of the culture that we grow up in will exercise an enormous attraction. Since we developed these programs for happiness before reason could provide any kind of moderation, they have no limits. When the desire for security is frustrated by some event and we cannot obtain the symbol of security that we desire, we immediately experience the afflictive emotions—grief, anger, jealousy, and so on.

The emotions faithfully identify the value system that developed in early childhood to cope with unbearable situations. These emotional programs for happiness start out as needs, grow into demands, and can finally become "shoulds." Others are then expected to respect our fantastic demands. People can grow up intellectually, physically, and even spiritually while their emotional lives remain fixated at the level of infancy, because they have never been able to integrate their emotions with the other values of their developing selves.

Persons whose emotional need for power and control has become a center of motivation like to control every situation and everyone. You may have met such persons in your family, or at work, or maybe in a religious community. Maybe you are one of them. In any case, such persons are programmed for human misery. In trying to control situations and other people, they are in competition with seven billion other people, many trying to do the same impossible thing. It can't possibly work; statistics are against them.

During the socialization period from ages four to eight, we absorb unquestioningly the values of our parents, teachers, and peer groups. We draw our identity or self-worth from what others in the particular group to which we belong think of us. Hence we have to measure up to their expectations. The emotional programs for happiness, already fully in place by age three or four, become much more complex. When we come to the age of reason and full reflective self-consciousness, we find ourselves at the most vulnerable point in our growth process. The human heart is designed for unlimited happiness—for limitless truth and for limitless love—and nothing less can satisfy. Hence we have to repress that desperate but unfulfilled hunger for happiness. We travel down various roads that promise happiness but can't provide it because they are only partial goods. Since the emotional programs from early childhood are already in place, our search for happiness in adult life tends to be programmed by childish expectations that cannot possibly be realized.

Here, for example, is a gentleman who has a hundred million dollars in assets. He is successful in Wall Street but not satisfied with his hundred million. He makes a million a day but still feels unsatisfied. He wants to make more money, and he wants to make more money so much that, although he already has a hundred million, he engages in fraudulent activity. His desire for more is insatiable. The nature of the emotional programs is to want to get more and more out of life, bigger and better pleasures, and more and more power over as many people as we can dominate, including God if we could get away with it. Most people are blissfully unaware that these emotional programs are functioning at full force inside them and secretly influencing their judgments and important decisions.

Again, someone who felt rejected in early childhood and never experienced real family life may be attracted to a religious community on the unconscious level, looking for a family he or she never had. Or children who feel deprived of affection may later choose spouses who they think can meet their dependency needs. If they choose mothers instead of wives or fathers instead of husbands, their marriages may be headed for serious trouble. This is not an impossible situation if they know what their problem is and take steps to deal with its dynamics. However, I have known people who were so dependent that they felt they could not escape from their ingrained over-dependence unless they actually separated from their spouses for a time. The dependency was so deep-rooted that it was reinforced just by living in the same house.

We come now to the heart of the problem of the human condition. Jesus addressed this problem head-on in the gospel. What was his first word when beginning his ministry? "Repent." To repent is not to take on afflictive penances like fasting, vigils, flagellation, or whatever else appeals to our generosity. It means *to change the direction in which you are looking for happiness.* That challenge goes to the root of the problem. It is not just a bandage for one or another of the emotional programs.

If we say yes to the invitation to repent, we may experience enormous freedom for a few months or for even a year or two. Our former way of life, in some degree, is cleaned up and certain relationships healed. Then, after a year or two the dust stirred up by our first conversion settles and the old temptations recur. As the springtime of the spiritual journey turns to summer—and fall and winter—the original enthusiasms begin to wane. At some point, we have to face the fundamental problem, which is the unconscious motivation that is still in place, even after we have chosen the values of the gospel. The false self is the syndrome of our emotional programs for happiness grown into sources of motivation and made much more complex by the socialization process, and reinforced by our overidentification with our cultural conditioning. Our ordinary thoughts, reactions, and feelings manifest the false self on every level of our conduct. When the false self learns that we have been converted and will now start practicing all the virtues, it has the biggest laugh of a lifetime and dares us, saying, "Just try it!"

Now we experience the full force of the spiritual combat, the struggle with what we want to do and feel we should do, and our incredible inability to carry it out. We recall Paul's classical lament:

> I don't understand myself at all. I really want to do what is right, but I can't. I do what I don't want to do—what I hate. I know perfectly well that what I am doing is wrong, and my bad conscience proves that I agree with these laws that I am breaking.. . . No matter which way I turn, I can't make myself do right. I want to, but I can't. When I want to do good, I don't; and when I try not to do wrong, I do it anyway. . . .

I love to do God's will, so far as my new nature is concerned. But there is something else deep within me, in my lower nature, that is at war with my mind, and wins the fight, and makes me a slave to sin that is still within me.. . . Oh, what a terrible predicament I am in! Who will free me from my slavery to this deadly lower nature? (Rom. 7:15–24, *The Living Gospel*)

Such insight is the beginning of the real spiritual journey. We realize, with a heavy heart, that it is going to be a long journey. We grasp that we are dealing with subtle forces that are powerful and fully in place. To dismantle these value systems in favor of the values of the gospel is not a matter of a few high spiritual experiences. These can remain merely tranquilizers of an exalted kind if we do not work to dismantle the false self and to practice the virtues. Spiritual highs give us temporary relief, but when they subside they leave us back where we were with all the same problems.

In this connection, two Greek New Testament words have special significance in Christian revelation.[1] *Sarx* is the body and the psyche locked into survival at its present level of human development. *Soma* is the body open to transcendence. *Sarx* is the "old Adam," Saint Paul's term for the false self, the ego bent on self-preservation at any cost, including other people's rights and needs. *Soma* is the new Adam with the transcendent element that Christ has brought into the human family by taking the entire human race to himself, thus giving it a decisive thrust toward wholeness and divine union. *Soma* is the emergence of full mental egoic consciousness and opens the way to further human development.

Shortly after Jesus was anointed by the Spirit in the River Jordan, he was led into the desert by the same Spirit to be tempted by the devil. Lent is our battle with the same temptations. The biblical desert symbolizes the confrontation with the false self and interior purification. Jesus was tempted regarding each one of the instinctual needs. He did not consent to them while yet experiencing them in their utmost intensity—"He was tempted in every way that we are, yet never sinned" (Heb. 4:15). When Jesus was desperately hungry, the devil maliciously suggested, "Why don't you change these stones into loaves of bread?" Jesus replied, "I choose to put my trust in Abba, my heavenly Father." Then the devil took him up to the pinnacle of the Temple and suggested that he jump off, sure of angelic protection, and thus be regarded as a wonder worker. Jesus rejected this appeal to fame out-of-hand. Finally the devil took him to the top of a high mountain and offered him power over all the nations of the world, saying, "If you bow down and worship me, you can have them all!" To this Jesus responded, "To hell with you!" Having rejected the exaggerated demands of each of the emotional programs for happiness, he invites us to do the same, saying, "Repent." This is as if he were to say, "Change the direction in which you are looking for happiness. You'll never find it in your emotional programs for happiness. Let go of your childish motivation because it can't possibly work in adult life."

Jesus' harsh sayings also cast a strong light on the false-self system. For instance, "If your eye scandalizes you, pull it out." Or, "If your hand or foot scandalizes you, cut it off." Obviously, these words are not to be taken literally. The Hebrew language uses exaggeration or the repetition of the same words to emphasize an important point. In this case, the point being stressed is our attachment to our emotional programs for happiness. We might thus paraphrase his words: "If your desire for survival/security, affection /esteem, and power/ control is so dear to you, as dear to you as your eye, or your hand or your foot, cut it off! This is the only way you can be free to enter the kingdom of God."

The heart of the Christian ascesis is the struggle with our unconscious motivations. If we do not recognize and confront the hidden influences of the emotional programs for happiness, the false self will adjust to any new situation in a short time and nothing is really changed. If we enter the service of the Church, the symbols of security, success, and power in the new milieu will soon become the new objects of our desires.

Thus the false self accompanies us, implacably, into whatever life-style we choose. Here is the story of a macho young man from a society in which drinking his friends under the table is the symbol of domination and success. He experiences enormous satisfaction as he watches his friends slithering under the table at the local tavern. Of course, this feeling of exaltation only lasts a few minutes, and he has to go to another tavern if he wants to enjoy the same result. Whatever satisfaction comes from getting what the false self wants is always brief.

This young man hears a televangelist and is totally converted from his evil ways. Not only is he resolved never to drink again; he isn't even going to eat an ice-cream cone. He looks around for the hardest religious order he can find, and, sure enough, he discovers the Trappists. "There," he thinks, "they scarcely eat anything." He applies to a monastery and is welcomed with open arms. He evidences that great spirit of austerity that the Trappists were especially strong on in those days. So he enters the monastery and dives into all the rules of strict silence and heavy work. Lent comes and the monks are fasting on bread and water. As the weeks pass, he notices the older brethren disappearing from the refectory. They are eating in the infirmary because their health has been weakened by the severe fast. Others are catching the flu. By Holy Week he is left alone in the refectory. As the great bell rings out for the Paschal Vigil, he staggers out of the refectory. To his surprise, he feels a familiar surge of pride and self-exaltation reminiscent of his former tavern accomplishments; only now, instead of drinking all his friends under the table, he has fasted all the monks under the table.

What, I ask you, has changed in this young man? Nothing apart from his address, hairdo, and clothes. This is what the gospel means by worldliness. When John says, "Leave the world," he does not mean the world with its desperate needs that cry out to be served. He means the self-centered projects, programs, demands—rationalized, justified, and even glorified—of security, pleasure, esteem, and power, which hinder our growing up into full human personhood. Persons who take responsibility for their emotions do not project their painful emotions on other people. In fact, even if we should succeed in manipulating other people and situations to our liking, nothing really changes, for the root of the problem is not in them but in us.

2

The False Self in Action

Minus the macho, that young man in the last chapter could have been myself. My conversion to Christ was extremely deep and personal prior to entering the monastery, and marked by a strong attraction for long periods of prayer and a willingness to make almost any sacrifice to follow Christ. Although there continued to be occasional periods of consolation in prayer, my early years in monastic community brought me face to face with the not-so-pleasant parts of myself, as I came to experience firsthand the false self in action. I knew that the Trappist life was going to be difficult. But what I expected would be difficult was not as hard as I expected. And what I expected would be easy proved to be difficult in the extreme.

I joined the monastic community because I was sold on the idea of spending my whole life in search of union with Christ. In my understanding, contemplative prayer was the heart of the spiritual journey. At the time, an austere regime was considered the indispensable way to contemplation; hence I looked for the most difficult order I could find. I was willing to give up everything—family, friends, and comfort—in order to follow Christ into the desert.

Newcomers to a Trappist monastery in the mid-1940s could normally speak only to the abbot and the novice master. Both had almost absolute authority over the novices, a fact that did not help to develop spontaneous relationships. The only communication allowed between the monks was a sign language limited to functional communication. As inheritors of the strict Trappist reform of the Cistercian Order instituted a century prior to the French Revolution, Trappists generally believed that the more silent you were and the more penances you performed, the closer you would draw to God and the more likely you were to make spiritual progress. Vocal prayers took up a significant part of the day. We rose ordinarily before two in the morning, an hour earlier on big feast days, and went to bed at seven at night. The work was frequently hard manual labor. The food was not very nourishing. The vegetables that we harvested in the fall were wrinkled and a bit soggy by March.

I bought into the rules hook, line, and sinker. The only way that I could survive was to get on my knees and beg God's help. I used to go to the church during every free moment, which added up to a couple of hours on most days. Since growth in contemplative prayer was my goal, I wanted to spend as much time as I could in the church. When praying privately in church, a monk was supposed to stand or kneel; sitting down was forbidden by the book of regulations. Although calluses were forming on my knees from kneeling so long, I hoped that if I persevered in extended periods of prayer, I would someday achieve my ideal of becoming a contemplative.

When I had been in the monastery for a year or so, another person entered the community who seemingly had the same idea. Like me, he came to church regularly during all the periods of free time, but he had the good sense to get permission from the abbot, who could dispense from certain regulations, to sit down during his prolonged visits. That possibility never occurred to me. I made a point of not allowing myself any relaxation in observing all the rules.

For months the newcomer spent as much time in church as I did. Often when I came in from work, washed up quickly, and hastened upstairs to kneel in church, he would be there. A general sense of uneasiness started to float through my mind along with my efforts to pray: I wondered how he was able to get here ahead of me. Whenever I took a furtive glance in his direction, he always seemed to have a beatific smile hovering about his lips. The thought came, "How is it that I am wearing out my knees while this guy who is always sitting down seems to be enjoying the Lord's special favors?"

I began to recognize that these thoughts were prompted by envy. Here I was in this holy place, in this holy position, trying to practice the holiest kind of prayer, and I was envying someone else's spiritual attainment. I had read enough about moral theology to know that this was the worst kind of envy. The thought came, "I was better before I came to this monastery. Maybe I should leave." This temptation went on for months, though not always with the same intensity. I even had thoughts that I should give up prayer altogether because whenever I tried these feelings of envy arose. Fortunately, I had enough sense to realize that I should not be governed by my own judgment in so important a matter. When I sought advice, our abbot encouraged me to persevere in prayer no matter what happened. As a man of prayer, he was aware of the purification that usually begins when one enters a life of strict silence, solitude, and prayer: one's mixed motivation emerges into clear awareness. Grace is there, but so is the false self.

The truth about ourselves is inevitable; whatever it is, it is going to come up. When the dust settles after the first fervor of religious conversion, we once again confront our old temptations. They may be worse than before because now we are more honest, open, and vulnerable. The great struggle is not to get discouraged when the divine reassurance begins to recede. It seems that God wants us to know experientially just what he has been putting up with throughout our lives. He seems to expect us to receive this information not as a reproach, but as a gift—like a friend revealing secrets to a friend. But instead of saying, "Thanks," we are ready to get up and walk out.

As I sat there day after day engulfed in horrible feelings of envy and praying for them to go away, matters got worse. Every now and then, especially on a bad day when I had been through other difficulties, these feelings translated into taste. I could virtually taste the feeling of envy in my mouth and would think to myself, "This is like sinking my teeth into a piece of juicy manure! And the manure is me!"

After three or four years of struggling with these feelings, I was thrown into a situation where I could speak with my brother monk. I discovered that he had the same problems I had in trying to find enough free time for prayer and that his periods of consoled prayer alternated with very heavy seas. As we sympathized with each other, my envy vanished and in time we became friends.

On the spiritual journey, there is usually someone in our family, business, or community whom we cannot endure, someone who has a genius for bringing out the worst in us. No matter what we do, we cannot seem to improve the relationship. This was the nature of my envy toward my brother monk. He had not done anything to cause it. God simply used him to reflect back to me what *my* problem was. Thus the person who gives us the most trouble may be our greatest gift from God.

In religious circles there is a cliché that describes the divine purification as "a battering from without and a boring from within." God goes after our accumulated junk with something equivalent to a compressor and starts digging through our defense mechanisms, revealing the secret corners that hide the unacceptable parts of ourselves. We may think it is the end of our relationship with God. Actually, it is an invitation to a new depth of relationship with God. A lot of emptying and healing has to take place if we are to be responsive to the sublime communications of God. The full transmission of divine life cannot come through and be fully heard if the static of the false self is too loud.

Once we start the spiritual journey, God is totally on our side. Everything works together for our good. If we can believe this, we can save ourselves an enormous amount of trouble. Purification of the unconscious is an important part of the journey. The decision to choose the values of the gospel does not touch the unconscious motivation that is firmly in place by age three or four, and more deeply entrenched by the age of reason. As long as the false self with its emotional programs for happiness is in place, we tend to appropriate any progress in the journey to ourselves.

The experience of God's love and the experience of our weaknesses are correlative. These are the two poles that God works with as he gradually frees us from immature ways of relating to him. The experience of our desperate need for God's healing is the measure in which we experience his infinite mercy. The deeper the experience of God's mercy, the more compassion we will have for others.

Why did I, a young man who had given up so much to come to the monastery, experience such strong feelings of envy? Evidently one of the programs in my unconscious was still in place. Was I using the time of prayer as a security blanket? Or again, since prayer before the Blessed Sacrament was held in great honor in our monastery, was I in competition with my brother monk, somewhat like the young man who fasted everyone under the table?

The work of following Christ is like working with a psychotherapist who has a clear insight into what is wrong with us. With incredible accuracy, God puts his finger on exactly the spot that needs attention at this precise time in our spiritual growth. If we are hanging on to one last shred of possessiveness, he comes along and says, often through some person or event, "Won't you give this to me?"

In the book of Deuteronomy, Moses compares God's training of his people to an eagle training an eaglet to fly. In ancient times it was believed that eaglets learned to fly by being pushed out of the nest, which was usually perched on the edge of a cliff. This is a marvelous image of what we feel is happening to us. God seems to push us into something that we feel totally incapable of doing. We wonder if he still loves us. Or again, he pushes us out of whatever nest we are in. Like the eaglet desperately flapping its wings, we seem to be heading straight for the abyss. But like the mother eagle, God swoops down and catches us just before we hit the rocks. This happens again and again until the eaglet learns to fly.

After we have been treated in this fashion a number of times, we too may realize that it is not as dangerous as we first believed. We begin to be content with these hair-raising escapes. We learn to trust God beyond our psychological experiences. And we become more courageous in facing and letting go of the dark corners of ourselves and begin to participate actively in the dismantling of our prerational emotional programs.

We cannot escape from the worldliness that is inside us, but we can acknowledge and confront it. The invitation to allow God to change our motivation from selfishness to divine love is the call to transforming union.

3

The Afflictive Emotions

As we begin the difficult work of confronting our own unconscious motivations, our emotions can be our best allies. The emotions faithfully respond to what our value system is—not what we would like it to be, or what we think it is. Our emotions are perfect recorders of what is happening inside; hence they are the key to finding out what our emotional programs for happiness really are.

In a certain area of Africa, the local planters have a way of catching monkeys that raid the banana plantations. The planters split a coconut in half, scoop out the insides, and replace them with a sweetmeat they know that monkeys love. The coconut is then sealed up, leaving just a slit like one in a mailbox to allow the monkey to slip its hand in sideways. The hunters then hide in the underbrush and wait for an unsuspecting monkey to come swinging through the trees. In due time one shows up, smells the sweetmeat, and cries out, "A treat for me!" It jumps down, picks up the coconut, slips its hand through the slit, and grasps the sweetmeat.

But when it tries to remove the sweetmeat, its fist will not fit through the slit. The hunters emerge from the bush and start coming closer. With ever-increasing intensity the monkey keeps pulling as hard as it can, but to no avail. The monkey is dimly aware that the hunters are approaching and that if it does not let go of the sweetmeat, it will be captured. But it can't quite free itself from its desire to possess its newfound treasure. So the hunters catch it, roast it, and eat it.

This is a parable of the human condition. There are times when we too are dimly aware that if we think about an insult or harbor a particular desire for one more second, we will be caught by one of our afflictive emotions. We do not want to be caught, but at the same time we want to relish for a few more seconds the particular desire or the thought of revenge. Then the hunters—the afflictive emotions— catch us, roast us, and eat us! All the monkey had to do was open its hand and let go; then it could have jumped into a tree and been off to freedom. All we have to do is open our minds and hearts and let go.

We can learn to recognize our emotional programs for happiness by the afflictive emotions they set off. Basically, these emotions might be reduced to anger, grief, fear, pride, greed, envy, lust, and apathy. If we have an emotional investment in the instinctual needs for survival/ security, affection/esteem, or power/ control, the events that frustrate these desires will inevitably set off one or another of the afflictive emotions.

The imagination and the emotions work like the intermeshing wheels of an old watch; if one wheel moves, the other has to move. Along with every emotional frustration, a commentary also arises drawn from our personal history or temperament. Through this interaction the feelings grow more intense and the commentaries more violent. Even though we know that the process is making us miserable, we cannot stop, like the monkey with his hand in the sweetmeat. The body reacts by pouring chemicals into the bloodstream to prepare for action. Each wheel feeds into the other at an accelerating rate until we are on an emotional binge that may go for hours, days, weeks, or even years.

For example, here is a man who has undertaken the spiritual journey and is determined to practice the moral virtues of justice, prudence, fortitude, and temperance. In other words, he has *consciously* chosen the values of the gospel. There happens to be a secretary at his place of work whom he cannot stand; their chemistries do not agree. He makes all kinds of resolutions to love this person. Nothing helps. After a particularly fruitful retreat, he determines to forgive everything in the past and never to get angry again.

On the first day back at work, he arrives at the office with this new determination and finds that the secretary has left her dirty golf socks on his desk. A few hours later, she spills coffee all over an important letter he has just completed, and it has to be done over. At lunchtime, she disappears for a couple of hours leaving him to handle all her phone calls and interviews. In the middle of the afternoon, she rushes in saying that she met her boyfriend at lunch and has to go to the beach for the weekend, and so would he please take care of her work for the rest of the day. Without waiting for an answer or saying a word of thanks, she departs.

With each blow, the afflicted man resists his rising feelings of indignation. The brain and nervous system, as we pointed out before, are like a vast biocomputer. Many computers today, given a command to erase a program, will say, "Do you really want to erase this program?" In virtue of his good resolutions, this man's biocomputer prints a similar question: "Are you sure you really want your program of indignation?" In response to each untoward event throughout the day, he replies, "No, I don't want the program."

It is now four o'clock in the afternoon. His reservoir of interior peace, established by the retreat and renewed during his early morning period of centering prayer, is bone dry. Once again the computerized question flashes on his inner screen of consciousness: "Are you sure you really want your program of indignation?"

This time his answer is almost a shout: "Yes, give me the whole program!" The red lights start flashing. The computer starts to grind

out the printout. Out pour all the disagreeable things he has ever
suffered at the hands of this woman. Next come all the disagreeable
people he has ever met, all the events that have ever upset him, all his
anger and feelings of revenge toward anyone, all programmed with
cross references and elaborate commentaries previously recorded in
his memory bank. Moreover, the commentaries, based on his tem-
peramental biases and personal history, are calibrated to respond to
his ascending levels of emotional intensity. As his indignation cre-
scendos into anger, the thought arises, "Why doesn't somebody fire
this woman?" This commentary turns his anger into rage. The next
commentary is, "Why doesn't God strike this woman with light-
ning?" This commentary turns his rage into fury. A state of temporary insanity takes over and he screams, "No, no! Let me strangle her
with my bare hands!"

The printout may go on for hours. Eventually he gathers up all the
papers and goes home in utter turmoil. His wife and children take
one look at his face and head for the doors and windows. The evening
is ruined. He cannot eat. He cannot sleep. He tries to look at TV,
pours himself a drink, calls a friend on the telephone. Everything
is a disaster. Finally he collapses on his bed and falls into a fitful
sleep. He rises in the morning with a terrible headache and a feeling of utter defeat. In despair he sighs, "Oh God, what went wrong?"
Indeed, what became of his conscious resolutions to be patient, kind,
and forgiving?

It does not occur to him that he may be experiencing emotional
turmoil because there is something seriously wrong with his unconscious value system. The facts of the situation and what might be an
appropriate response are overwhelmed by the intensity of emotion
generated by the emotional programs for happiness in his unconscious. He projects the cause of his pain on the other person, saying, "If only I could get rid of her, how happy I would be!" And after

each emotional storm he wonders, "Why do people treat me this way? What have I done to deserve this?" Each time he gives in to his emotional programs and their expression, he is reborn into the endless cycle of desire, gratification, frustration, and the ensuing need to compensate.

This man has to modify his outrageous reactions and the value systems they reflect, if he is to begin to deal with the real problems that his coworker presents. Not every method is adequate or sufficiently comprehensive to deal with the subtleties of the false self. We need to choose one that is suitable for our state of life. We may also require some psychotherapy. Regular periods of centering prayer are the keystone of the whole program; they need to be reinforced by positive efforts in daily life to change our inveterate habits of acting under the influence of the emotional programs for happiness.

But having acknowledged the essential character of efforts to change, we must emphasize what Paul pointed out in the passage from Romans: The conscious resolution to change our values and behavior is not enough to alter the unconscious value systems of the false self and the behavior they engender. Only the passive purifications of contemplative prayer can effect this profound healing. Only then will the reservoir of interior silence, built up in periods of centering prayer, never run dry.

This man's experience, of course, is a paradigm of everyone's experience on the spiritual journey, given a little time for the process to develop. Whenever an emotional program is frustrated, we immediately experience a spontaneous feeling reaction. If something happens that undermines our need for a particular security symbol, the feeling of grief or anger instantly arises. When, for example, we arrive at work and the manager tells us that the other employees have been complaining about us and to look for another job, our instant reaction may be the feeling of hurt. Then the commentary promptly arises, "Who did this to me?" or "What will this look like on my resume?" After one or two self-protective thoughts like this, the churning sensation accelerates.

Let us try to identify the principal emotions or combinations of emotions that announce the presence of false-self values in the unconscious. Anger responds to goods that are difficult to obtain or evils that are hard to avoid. When something perceived in this way overtakes us, we experience anger.

Apathy is pervasive boredom or bitterness resulting from recurrent frustration. It is the withdrawal from life, friendship, and community. Someone who suffers this disease might complain, "I've served this community for twenty years. You've never asked my opinion. Or if you did, you never followed it. I'm going to my room and closing the door. Don't anyone dare to knock on that door. You go your way, I'm going mine." The bottom line is, "To hell with you!" Nobody can talk to such persons because they are hurt and self-righteous, and they love it. The latter feeling nourishes their sense of self-satisfaction because they hope that their withdrawal will hurt everyone else. It does. Thus they have their revenge. Apathy is the opting out of the flow of life in order to hug one's wounds, real or imaginary.

Lust in the context of the frustration of the emotional programs refers not just to sexual misbehavior. It is the overweening desire for satisfaction, whether physical, mental, or spiritual, in order to compensate for the intolerable affronts that people have inflicted on us by not honoring our unreasonable demands. As we saw, the emotional programs gradually grow into centers of motivation around which our thoughts, feelings, and behavior circulate like planets around the sun.

Pride as an emotional reaction may be experienced in two ways. Some people experience it as self-rejection instead of self-inflation. They have to punish themselves for not measuring up to their idealized images of themselves. Instead of being angry at other people for hurting their feelings, they turn the anger against themselves and say, "I'm no good." They may even adopt self-destructive measures if the emotion becomes strong enough. They cannot bear to see themselves failing because then pride brings down the verdict of guilty. Pride, not God, suggests that they never measure up to the demands that their idealized images impose upon them. On the other hand, if they succeed in something, their self-inflation, pride and variety can hardly be contained.

Any upsetting emotion is warning us that an emotional program may just have been frustrated. The cause may not be somebody else's misconduct or an unpleasant event. For us to be habitually happy, nobody has to change except ourselves. If we are upset by anything, we have a problem, and we will continue to experience emotional turmoil until we change the root of the problem, which is the emotional program for happiness in the unconscious. The effort to change it is called the practice of virtue.

If we keep our desires and aversions dried out by not watering them with commentaries or acting them out, they wither like weeds in the desert.

A certain businessman used to commute to work every day on the New York subway. He regularly stopped at a newsstand along the way to buy the *New York Times* to read on the train. One day a business associate accompanied him. When they came to the newsstand, the businessman said to the attendant, "Will you kindly give me a copy of the *New York Times?*" The attendant grabbed a copy and threw it at him.

The businessman said, "Thank you. Please accept your money." The attendant grabbed the money and thrust it into the cash register with a loud grunt. The businessman said, "I wish you a very good day." The attendant glared at him and responded, "I hope you have the worst day of your life!" With that he spat right in his direction. Undisturbed, our friend walked off toward the subway. His companion, who had been getting more and more exasperated finally burst out, "How can you put up with such treatment? I wouldn't stand for it for one moment. I would walk to the other side of town to catch the train rather than be treated in such an outrageous manner!" His friend replied, "Look, I have to take the subway to work every day. That newsstand is right on my way. Why should I inconvenience myself because of the way this person treats me?"

There is no commandment that says we have to be upset by the way other people treat us. The reason we are upset is because we have an emotional program that says, "If someone is nasty to me, I cannot be happy or feel good about myself." It is true that there is psychological and sometimes physical pain involved in not being treated as a human being. In such situations, we have every right to be indignant and to take steps to remedy them. But apart from such circumstances, instead of reacting compulsively and retaliating, we could enjoy our freedom as human beings and refuse to be upset.

Once on the spiritual journey, we begin to perceive that our emotional programs for happiness prevent us from responding to other people and their needs. When locked into our private worlds of narcissistic desires, we are not present to the needs of others when they seek help. The clarity with which we see other people's needs and respond to them is in direct proportion to our interior freedom.

4

The Human Condition

Personal sin is the ripe fruit of the emotional programs for happiness; it is not the chief problem, but the chief symptom of the problem. And the problem itself is clearly universal. It affects the entire human condition. In fact, it *is* the human condition.

The human condition is my term for the doctrine Christian tradition has referred to, since Saint Augustine of Hippo first proposed it, as original sin and its consequences. No theologian ever considered original sin the personal fault of any one of us. It was strictly reserved as the sin of our first parents. The doctrine of the Fall was an effort on the part of theologians to explain how the pervasive disease of human nature came about. Taoism, Hinduism, Buddhism, and other religions also bear witness to the experience of a universal illness that has afflicted the human family from the beginning.

Psychology is evidently coming to a similar conclusion regarding the pervasiveness of this disease. In fact, one of the great benefits of contemporary psychology is the precision that it provides regarding the nature and causes of the human condition as we experience it. The discovery of the unconscious by Freud a little over a hundred years ago has immense significance for the spiritual life. It means that most of our faults and their causes are hidden from us. More recently, the literature about the dysfunctional family and co-dependency provides us with a diagnosis of the human condition far more detailed than that provided by the doctrine of the consequences of original sin and the capital sins that we learned about in catechism class. The science and practice of psychology greatly reinforce all that we previously understood about the dynamics of human motivation and hence are essential for moral judgments. Thus psychology has become the new "handmaid of theology." At the same time it gives new validation to the earlier insights gained through theological reflection on revelation and through contemplative prayer.

We have seen already in the first chapter how one such model—the developmental, pioneered by child psychologist Jean Piaget—helps explain the roots of our unconscious emotional programs for happiness. Each of us needs to be reassured and affirmed in his or her own personhood and self-identity. If this assurance is withheld because of lack of concern or commitment on the part of parents, these painful privations will require defensive or compensatory measures. As a consequence, our emotional life ceases to grow in relation to the unfolding values of human development and becomes fixated at the level of the perceived deprivation. The emotional fixation fossilizes into a program for happiness. When fully formed it develops into a center of gravity, which attracts to itself more and more of our psychological resources: thoughts, feelings, images, reactions, and behavior. Later experiences and events in life are all sucked into its gravitational field and interpreted as helpful or harmful in terms of our basic drive for happiness. These centers, as we shall see, are reinforced by the culture in which we live and the particular group with which we identify, or rather, overidentify.

The developmental model is actually a subset of an even more comprehensive model, the evolutionary. The infant experiences the same developmental pattern and value systems that the human family as a whole experienced. In other words, each human being is a microcosm of where the human race has been—and where it might be headed. For the evolutionary model I will follow the insightful arrangement of Ken Wilber, which he calls the Great Chain of Being.[1]

Some five million years ago, the first flicker of differentiation between animal and human life took place with the development in humans of what is now termed "reptilian consciousness." The mythological symbol of this consciousness is the serpent eating its tail, signifying the recurrence of natural processes: day and night, summer and winter, birth and death, desire and satisfaction. The most primitive humans were totally immersed in nature. They had no consciousness of a separate self. Their lives were centered on day-to-day survival activities such as the search for food and shelter and on the prompt fulfillment of instinctual needs.

The infant in the first year of life experiences reptilian consciousness and is totally immersed in matter and pleasurable sensations. The first year is an experience of unity with the mother and continuity with the life once enjoyed in the womb. If bonding with the mother takes place right away, the baby is on the road to accepting emotionally the human adventure.

About two hundred thousand years ago, reptilian consciousness moved into "typhonic consciousness." This awareness was embedded in animal life and primitive instincts, but it enabled these new humans to distinguish their bodies from other objects in the environment. This type of consciousness is usually expressed in mythology by the symbol of the Typhon, the part-human, part-animal creature, aware of a body-self but dominated by its instincts for survival, nourishment, and reproduction. Typhonic culture revolved around hunting and worship of the Great Earth Mother as nurturer and protectress.

The characteristics of typhonic consciousness are manifested by the infant between the ages of two and four. The infant experiences his body-self as separate from the objects in the environment and from his siblings. Supported by the newly developing capacity of the brain to process sensory information at a rapid rate, the child wants to explore her world and try things out. The child's consciousness participates in the part-human, part-animal world of typhonic consciousness. Her dreams are mostly about animals or animal images that personify people. The dreamlike quality of typhonic consciousness is manifested in a child's games and imagery. A block can represent a car and a closet becomes a spaceship in which to travel to the stars or to the center of the earth. A young child cannot clearly distinguish imagination from reality or the part from the whole; anything she can imagine exists or can happen. Children also suffer from the terrors that were typical of our typhonic ancestors: the dark, the unknown, the powers of nature, and the monsters created by the imagination.

The move from typhonic to "mythic membership" consciousness, accelerated by the invention of language, occurred around 12,000 B.C.E. The invention of farming facilitated this movement by providing leisure for art, reflection, ritual, and politics. The stratification of society in the form of city-states led to the acquisition of land and possessions and the struggle to defend or extend them by wars of ever-increasing proportions. At the mythic membership level, identification with the community provided the sense of belonging, protection from enemies, and the prolongation of one's life through offspring. The social self, identified with a particular city-state or family grouping, developed hierarchies for ritual sacrifice, the authority of kings and nobles, and slavery to serve the cultural expansion of the victors in war. As people became more self-conscious and hence capable of anticipating death, they sought to hide their growing fear of it. They projected into the future a life that they could not, in fact, be sure of. Ways of forgetting the proximity of death, according to some anthropologists, are one of the main thrusts in the formation of cultures.[2]

Between the fourth and eighth year, the child enters the period of socialization and accesses the mythic membership level of consciousness where possessions, competition, success, belonging to a group, and interiorizing the values of a structured society are the order of the day. The child at this age absorbs unquestioningly the values of parents, teachers, peers, and the predominant society in which he is being raised.

About 3000 B. C. E. the most dramatic leap in human consciousness took place: the emergence of reason. This level of consciousness is termed by anthropologists "mental egoic" and is symbolized in Greek mythology by Zeus slaying the dragon. Zeus represents reason; the dragon stands for the domination of the emotions and primitive levels of consciousness.

Theoretically, to continue with this paradigm, the mental egoic is the era we live in now, and the level of consciousness that we attain in the normal course of our human development after about eight years of age. It would be comforting if this were so. Then the human condition might be not a pervasive illness but a right evolution toward ever-greater participation in the possibilities of life. Unfortunately, this is not the case. For along with the emergence of full reflective self-consciousness and the sense of personal identity, there also arose a growing sense of separation from God. If humankind had enjoyed the awareness of divine union as the levels of consciousness unfolded, the emergence of full reflective self-consciousness would not have been experienced as threatening. But instead, the developing levels of consciousness brought a growing sense of alienation from God, oneself, others, and the cosmos.

Mental egoic consciousness is the movement beyond the self-centered instinctual drives and gratifications of the prerational instincts into full personhood. It is to take responsibility for ourselves as well as to respond to the needs of our families, our nations, and the human race, including the generations yet to come. But this level of consciousness is still not accessed by the vast majority of humankind. For, as we have seen, the human condition is still under the sway of the false self with its emotional programs for happiness based on the primitive stages of consciousness: security from the reptilian, affection/esteem and power/control from the typhonic. As a result, even as adults our consciousness is still in many respects infantile. And culture as a whole has not advanced beyond the mythic membership level, as we shall see in chapter ten, whose values the gospel specifically challenges.

In the reptilian and the typhonic periods of the evolutionary journey of the human family, the Great Earth Mother personified the paradisiacal innocence that remains as an archetype in every human being. Since each stage of human evolution is recapitulated in each one of us, we dimly recall how pleasant it was to be immersed in nature and to enjoy the animal functions of eating and reproducing without accountability. There is an unconscious tendency in every human being to regress to the bliss of the womb; we naturally prefer to regress to a place that was familiar rather than to go forward into the unknown.

Every movement of human growth precipitates a crisis appropriate to the level of physical, emotional, or spiritual development at which we find ourselves. Each major crisis of growth requires letting go of the physical or spiritual food that has been nourishing us up to then and moving into more mature relationships. In such a crisis we tend to seek the feeling of security. It is characteristic of reptilian and typhonic consciousnesses to react to frustration by choosing the line of least resistance, or whatever seems to be the easiest security blanket in which to wrap themselves. The capacity to go forward into personal responsibility is constantly challenged by the temptation to revert to lower levels of consciousness and behavior. Human growth is not the denial or rejection of any level, but the integration of the lower into more evolved levels of consciousness.

Human development depends on freeing ourselves from emotional fixations on these instinctual levels in order to grow to full reflective self-consciousness. The gospel calls for the full development of the human person and invites us to the further growth that God has in store for us: the intuitive and unitive levels of consciousness to which mature faith and love gradually raise us. Meanwhile, passing through the mythic membership stage to the mental egoic stage, we feel the undertow of primitive instincts. They remain part of us until they are thoroughly integrated by the purification of sense and spirit from the influences of the emotional programs for happiness.

At the same time, we have a vague remembrance that somewhere, back in the reptilian period, everything was unified. Indeed, during that period, there was no consciousness of a separate self, no sense of accountability. There was a mysterious wholeness. This is the experience of innocence symbolized by the Garden of Eden. As adults we yearn for the kind of un-selfconscious unity that was actually present in the first year or two of life, but was lost during the development of the separate-self sense. It is to be recovered in an immensely superior form in the transforming union.

5

Mythic Membership Consciousness

Overidentification with the group is the dominant characteristic of mythic membership consciousness. When we derive our identity from the social unit of which we are a member, we give the group unquestioning loyalty. The sense of belonging to something important gives us feelings of security, pleasure, and power. A child may boast to his companions, "My daddy is better than your daddy." Believing that his daddy can beat up anybody on the block supports the child's need to feel secure in relating to the broader community.

The uncanny ability of an established group to resist constructive change is supported by the overidentification of its members. The first group we come in contact with is the family. There is nothing wrong with experiencing loyalty to our roots, but the influence of the emotional programs exaggerate what is reasonable in our loyalty. Peer-group pressure demands conformity whether or not our consciences fully approve of what is being done. As we identify with the group's value system, we conform more easily and resist those who challenge the group on any point. Thus conformity patterns become entrenched.

When authority functions on the mythic membership level, it easily moves from the exercise of authority to authoritarianism.

Jesus' idea of authority belongs to the mental egoic level. Authority is designed to serve those whom it leads. It is exercised to elicit and encourage the creativity of the members of the Christian community. Authority in the Christian religion is designed to lead us out of the swamp of self-centered motivation into the freedom and account-ability of full personhood. We can then take our place in the mystical body of Christ as a living cell responsible for the well-being of the whole body.

Jesus directs strong words to people at the mythical membership level: "If anyone comes to me without turning his back on his father and mother, his wife and his children, his brothers and sisters, indeed his very self, he cannot be my follower" (Luke 14:26). It is important to grasp the force of this saying. We can be sure he does not mean that we should cease to love or care for our parents. In Jesus' time it was the custom to make contributions to the Temple in place of sup-porting one's parents in their old age, a practice Jesus vigorously con-demned. The text urges us to refuse to be locked into a conformity that prevents us from following the values of the gospel. As we grow, our relationships to ourselves, God, and other people change. We start life dependent on our parents, but in adulthood our relation-ship changes to one of equality. The old relationship of dependency dies and we form a new relationship. We continue to love them, but if they want us to do something against our values, we must be able to say, "I love you, but I can't go along with you in this matter."

The same thing goes for membership in a broader group. We may have to say, "I can't remain a member." If family, nation, or group—anyone—stands in the way of our true growth, which is in the inter-est of the whole human family, we have to be able to say "no" and stick to it. We may lose a few friends by modifying our way of life, because they may find the change in us threatening. The spiritual journey can be a lonely road in the beginning. Later God will give

us new friends. God does not take anything away except to give us
something better.

A significant influence in the life of the developing human being
is the superego, which is an emotional judgment of what is right
or wrong behavior. Parents and teachers give the child "do's" and
"don'ts" which may be accompanied by punishments or threats.
The precepts in themselves may have no real moral significance.
The superego, however, treats them as "shoulds," and they become
a source of guilt feelings. Later in life, when a true conscience that
belongs to the age of reason is formed, we have to struggle with these
parental injunctions, especially if they were laced with sanctions.
Thus a significant part of genuine moral development consists in
freeing ourselves from the tyranny of the superego. This is not to
reject all the values we have received up to that point, but rather to
reevaluate them, putting moral injunctions into the broader perspective of our relationship with God.

Some adolescents rebel against the moral straitjackets in which
they were raised. The only path to freedom apparent to them may
be to throw the whole thing over. If religious values have been inter-
twined with a tyrannical superego, there will be a reaction against a
religion that was presented in an overmoralistic way. It may look as
though these adolescents have given up their religion, but they may
be simply struggling against heavy odds to make their own judgments about religious values. It may take a long time, however, for
their rebellion to subside.

Ideas about morality may or may not be the result of a right conscience. At the height of the conflict in Northern Ireland, Catholic
children were inculcated from birth to hate Protestants and vice
versa. They grew up with the same hatred that their mothers, fathers,
grandparents, and great-grandparents cherished. Imagine the guilt
feelings that would arise if a Catholic fell in love with a Protestant.

Such a couple would feel they were betraying their respective religions and families. This is the superego at work making an emotional judgment regarding right and wrong. A true conscience functions on the basis of reason and faith.

Much of the spiritual journey consists in getting rid of the effects of the superego. Could anything be more frightening to a child than to hear that one mortal sin could catapult him into hell forever? The child unquestioningly receives religious instruction from parents and teachers. He does not evaluate the information about God or the way the information is given—or if he does, he tries to find ways of coping with disturbing information.

A five-year-old in a certain household began acting strangely. Whenever he was asked a question, he would say, "I don't know."

"Did you brush your teeth?"

"I don't know."

"Did you have breakfast?"

"I don't know."

"Did you kiss Mommy goodnight?"

"I can't remember."

The household thought it was a great joke, but after a while his conduct began to get on their nerves. His alert grandma finally intervened. "There's something wrong with this child," she said. "Take him to a psychiatrist."

The doctor discovered that the boy's nurse had said to him, "A lie is a mortal sin. If you tell one, you will go to hell." The youngster felt that he could not always be certain whether what he said was true or not, so he decided not to take any chances—and was well on the way to becoming thoroughly neurotic. This nurse thought she was faithfully reflecting the moral teaching of her religion, but if her admonitions had not been stopped, she would have caused permanent emotional damage to that child and retarded his spiritual growth, perhaps for good, by casting deep shadows on his relation-ship with God.

Let me give another example of how the superego works. When I entered the austere life of the monastery, fasting was held in honor. When I completed my formation and was given the job of novice master, I wanted to set a good example of fidelity for the novices. The symbol of fidelity in a monastery in those days was perfect conform-ity to the rule. This meant being on time for all the offices, perform-ing manual labor, and observing the fasts. Because I was somewhat fragile in health, I rarely was able to get through the whole of Lent without having to be dispensed from the fasting. In the milieu of the monastery, if one could not fast, one felt like a second-class citizen. One Lent I approached the abbot to ask permission to start the fast even though I had always been forced to drop out after a couple of weeks. To my surprise he said, "Do you want to know the penance that God wants you to do this Lent?" I said, "Sure." His response was, "Gain twenty pounds." In order to reinforce this injunction, he added, "Between meals, each morning and afternoon, I want you to drink a glass of cream and eat two Hershey bars."

My first thought was, "Has the abbot gone mad? Does he think this is a country club?" Notice the commentary rising out of my hurt feelings and monastic superego. With a heavy heart, I withdrew from his office and reluctantly started this unusual Lenten observance.

My next thought was, "How am I going to prevent the novices from knowing about this?" I did not want them to lose confidence in my austere leadership. But there was no escape. I had to throw all self-respect to the winds. They fasted and I did not. I faithfully drank cream and ate two Hershey bars between meals every day during Lent and actually gained ten pounds.

The great gift that the abbot gave me was not the ten pounds, but his insightful perception that I was attached to the observance of fasting in a way that was not wholesome. The peculiar penance that he imposed freed me from my overidentification with what I had interiorized as the proper way to be a monk and especially a monastic superior. We all have notions of the proper way to be a husband, wife, father, mother, employee, or employer, and a proper way to be a member of our parish or religious community. These preconceived ideas lock us into one way of doing things. This is what I mean by overidentification with the values of our group. Our preconceived ideas and prepackaged value systems are obstacles to grace. Centering prayer increases our inner freedom, enabling us to reevaluate them in the light of the gospel.

I appeal to your own experience. Recall the undertow of guilt feelings when you tried to break out of your parental value system or early religious instruction. True guilt is the realization that you have acted against your conscience; that is to say, that you have done something against what you believe is right. The sense of guilt warns you, "Hey, you have gone against your principles." As soon as you regret your fault and say, "My God, forgive me," you should forget it. Guilt feelings that last longer than half a minute are neurotic. Pervasive, prolonged, and paralyzing guilt is the result of the super-ego at work. It is an emotional judgment about right and wrong, not a true judgment of conscience. Neurotic pride says, "Look what you've done! You're just no good!" It accuses us not only of having done wrong in a particular instance, but of being totally worthless. When we do not measure up to our self-images, pride brings down the verdict of guilty, and we mistakenly project that judgment onto God. Meanwhile, God is saying, "There's nothing seriously wrong with you. Everybody makes mistakes. Forget it." Or, "I forgive you. Why don't you forgive yourself?"

Loyalty to family, country, and religion, and gratitude for all the good we have received from them is a virtue, but loyalty is not an absolute value. It should be enlightened by mental egoic conscious-ness. This more mature level of consciousness presupposes personal responsibility for the community in which we live insofar as we can influence it for good.

The structures of government that belong to the mythic member-ship level of consciousness are mostly monarchical, dictatorial, and authoritarian in form. The mental egoic level of consciousness, since it involves personal responsibility for the group, is inclined toward participatory forms of government in which a broad constituency of qualified people are consulted. The final decision is thus enlightened by all the facts. In our time, the facts are more and more complex. Experts need to be consulted in important matters before a final judg-ment is taken if any decision is going to be an adequate one today.

6

Attitudes Towards God

One of the chief factors that tend to destroy relationships among people and nations is the emotion of fear. It also destroys the relationship between us and God. To be afraid of God, or to be afraid of other people, makes us defensive. In the case of God, we will try to stay as far away from him as our situations and the demands of respectability permit. In the case of other people, we try to control them and hold them within limits that enable us to feel secure.

The biblical term "fear of God" does not refer to the emotion of fear. Fear of God is a technical term in the Bible meaning the right relationship with God. The right relationship with God is to trust him. The right relationship with God involves reverence and awe for God's transcendence and immanence as well as trust in his goodness and compassion. To envisage what the biblical fear of God actually means, imagine a child at Christmas time in a huge department store. The top floor, the size of a whole city block, is filled with toys. When the child emerges from the elevator into this wonderland of desirable objects, her eyes grow bigger and bigger. She looks to the left and to the right, seeing everything her heart has ever desired: skis, T-bears, doll houses, toys, sleds, electric trains, computers. She wants to go in every direction at once. She is so enthralled that she does not know where to start. She wants to grasp everything and take it home. The biblical fear of God is similar. We feel ourselves invited into a mystery that contains everything our hearts could possibly desire. We experience the fascination of the Ultimate Mystery rather than fear of the unknown. We want to grasp or be grasped by the mystery of God's presence that opens endlessly in every direction.

Here is an incident that might emphasize this point. It is a story told on himself by Cardinal Basil Hume, the Primate of England. As a youngster, he was brought up in a strict English household. Wanting to discipline the children, his mother called them together one day and, pointing to a jar in the pantry, said, "You see that cookie jar? I don't want you children putting a hand in that jar between meals. It is only for dessert on feast days." And as a sanction she added: "Because God is always watching you." Naturally, the children were shaking in their shoes. Young Basil's idea of God, which had been very trusting up to that point, shifted to that of a policeman always watching for his every fault. This unhealthy fear of God seems to have retarded his spiritual growth for the next twenty or thirty years.

Parents and teachers, despite good intentions, sometimes project onto God sanctions of their own creation. God only gave us ten commandments. Let us not add any more. If people want to impose more commandments, they should blame themselves, not God.

Young Basil eventually entered the Benedictine order. There were more rules there than his mother had laid down at home. I suppose he kept them for the same reason: fear of this God ever on the watch to catch him in some fault. If I had been the vocation director when this young man presented himself at the monastery, I would have been tempted to ask him, "What is your motive for coming here? You are giving up family, friends, career, and all the other things your brilliant mind could do. Are you sure that your primary motive may not be to placate the God that you heard about in childhood and whom you identified as a policeman, a tyrant, and pitiless judge? . . ."

"One day," the cardinal said in concluding his story, "I received a very special grace that completely changed my attitude toward God. I realized that if as a child I had put my hand in the cookie jar, and if it had been between meals, and if God had really been watching me, he would have said, 'Son, why don't you take another one?'"

This, I submit, is the God of the Christians. I do not know this other god, and don't want to know him. Such a god is a caricature of the true God. Such a god is certainly not the God of Jesus Christ, whom he called "Abba," the God of infinite concern for everyone, ever present to us and enfolding us in his infinite love. That is what a child needs to hear.

7

Mental Egoic Consciousness

We saw in the first five chapters how the gospel calls us to grow to full personhood, to grow out of our childish programs for happiness, necessary for survival during the fragile period of childhood but now an obstacle to becoming fully human. We saw as well how the gospel invites us to disidentify with the values of our cultural conditioning, whether ethnic, nationalistic, or even religious, insofar as these values hinder our personal response to Christ.

Given the prepackaged values firmly entrenched from early childhood, the arising of mental egoic consciousness at about the age of reason finds us unfree to reevaluate our enormous emotional and social investment in prerational attitudes. Thus we use our newfound intellectual powers to rationalize, justify, and even glorify our emotional programs and the false values of the culture.

Instead of developing the capacity to relate to other persons and to all reality with honesty and compassion, we use the immensely creative energy of rational consciousness to develop more sophisticated ways of controlling people, extracting greater pleasures out of life, and heaping up more security symbols. Thus we reinforce the self-centered motivation appropriate to childhood but totally inappropriate for adults.

Our pathology is simply this: we have come to full reflective self-consciousness without the enjoyment of divine union—indeed, without any awareness of it at all. Because that crucial conviction, born of experience, is missing, our fragile egos seek every possible means to ward off the painful and at times agonizing sense of alienation from God and from everyone else. As we saw, the poignant character of this sense of alienation from God is described by Augustine as the consequences of original sin.

In the story of the Garden of Eden there is a charming reference to God conversing with Adam and Eve in the cool of the evening, a lively image of intimacy with the divine and harmony with the powers of nature. This, the true garden of paradise, is not primarily a place but a state of consciousness. As long as intimacy with God was enjoyed by our first parents, everything in creation was friendly. As soon as that intimacy was lost, briars grew up instead of crops and all the ills of fallen human nature came upon them.

These images reflect what we experience in our own psychological awareness. We come to full reflective self-consciousness without the easy intimacy with God that Adam and Eve enjoyed in the garden. We lack a sense of oneness with God, other people, and the cosmos. We feel incomplete and afraid and hence seek symbols of security, affection, and power to shore up our fragile self-identities.

When the gospel of John proclaims, "The word became flesh," the author is indicating that God took upon himself not human nature in its ideal state before the Fall, but human nature in its actual condition of privation, sin, and death.

Jesus on the cross is a striking symbol of the human condition when it reaches the mental egoic state of consciousness: we cannot regress to primal innocence and the irresponsibility of animal life, and we cannot rise under our own power to higher states of consciousness. We feel rejected, as it were, by both heaven and earth—like Jesus, crucified between heaven and earth. Jesus urges his disciples not to regress to earlier stages of consciousness, but to go forward into full personhood, to assume full responsibility for ourselves and our relationships, and to open to the Ultimate Reality whom he called Abba, Father.

Similarly, Jesus invites us to change the direction in which we are looking for happiness and to join the new humanity that is opening to interior freedom and self-transcendence. The primary issue for the human family at its present level of evolutionary development is to become fully human. But that, as we have seen, means rediscovering our connectedness to God, which was repressed somewhere in early childhood.

The arrival at the mental egoic stage of consciousness is characterized by basic attitudinal changes. One graduates from mere self-concern and is motivated by the larger concerns of family, country, and the world. In mythic membership consciousness our concern for others is principally motivated by personal security, esteem, and power considerations. Our personal identity is associated with our group affiliation and its response to us. The mental egoic level begins to manifest itself when the powers of the brain have developed biologically to the point of sustaining abstract thinking, somewhere around twelve to fourteen years of age. This new level of relating is established only with difficulty, because the lower levels with their value systems and selfish motivations are firmly in place and resist change in the sense of growth.

Jesus expressed this level and called everyone to it when he reaffirmed the first commandment of the Mosaic Law and stated that the second was like to it: "You shall love your neighbor as yourself." In philosophical language this first commandment means that we must respect the rights and needs of others. This was the starting point of the teaching of Jesus. His own second commandment, "Love one another as I have loved you," goes much further and presupposes a movement to higher levels of motivation.

The mental egoic level is the level of the full emergence of moral responsibility for our behavior and relationships. It is the level of true conscience, the capacity to distinguish rightly and not just notionally, between right and wrong. Hence personal sin becomes much more serious. Basically, personal sin is the ratification of the emotional programs for happiness and the values of our cultural conditioning insofar as they disregard the rights and needs of others and our own true good.

The dispositions proper to the mental egoic level reflect the growing sense of equality with other humans, accountability for the care and preservation of the earth and its living and inorganic resources, and a more mature relationship to God. Respect for others diminishes the drive to dominate and control. Cooperation replaces unbridled competition. Harmony replaces rigid value systems. Negotiating replaces exclusive self-interest or national interests. Living in peace with others becomes a more important value, though not at any price. Accessing full mental egoic consciousness is the door leading to the great adventure of recovering and developing union with God.

In this adventure, further human growth begins with the intuitive level of consciousness. The good dispositions planted in the mental egoic stage begin to bloom. The sense of belonging to the universe and being one with others takes root. Compassion moves beyond respect for the rights and needs of others. The activity of the intuitive brain increases; there are more frequent insights, spiritual consolations, and psychic gifts. But the false self can still co-opt these gifts and turn them into ego trips and motives for spiritual pride; hence the need for the purification of the unconscious and the growth of self-knowledge in order to discern the subtle workings of our emotional programs from the movements of the Spirit.

8

The Four Consents

O ur instinctual needs gradually grew into emotional programs
for happiness because in growing up we had no experience of
the divine presence within, which is the true security, the deepest
affirmation of our basic goodness, and the true freedom. Since we
did not even know that God was actually present within us, we had
to look elsewhere for the security, affirmation, and freedom that only
the divine presence can provide. The spiritual journey is a training
in consent to God's presence and to all reality. Basically this is what
true humility is. The divine action invites us to make the consents
that we were unable to make in childhood and growing up because
of the circumstances that surrounded our early lives.

This brings us to a paradigm for the spiritual journey that sheds
a great deal of light on the positive aspects of grace, which not only
heals the emotional damage of a lifetime, but also empowers us to
enter on the path of unconditional love, even from the beginning
of our conversion. Jesus emphasized this approach to divine union
when he said, "Love one another as I have loved you."

The theologian John S. Dunne has suggested that the stages of the
spiritual journey correspond to the passage of human life from birth
to death.[1] At each major stage of that development, God asks us to
make an appropriate consent. Let us follow closely Dunne's insightful presentation.

In childhood, God asks us to consent to the basic goodness of our nature with all its parts. As children we experience our own faculties, develop imagination, memory, and language, and learn to relate to family and peers. In these years we are asked to accept the basic goodness of our being as a gift from God and to be grateful for it. The acceptance of our basic goodness does not refer to what we can do or do better than others, but to the goodness of our being before we do anything.

Unfortunately, if our childhood environment is filled with fear, rejection, or ambivalent signals of parental affection and caring, or if we are burdened with some physical handicap, our emotions may hesitate to give full consent to the goodness of life. The biological need to survive usually gets us through this hesitation. We develop ways to bolster our fragile self-images and to go on living, but we bring our ambivalence toward life into the next stage.

In early adolescence, God asks us to accept the full development of our being by activating our talents and creative energies. Puberty actualizes the physical side of a much broader energy: our capacity to relate to other people, to emerge out of the isolated world of a child, and to begin to assume responsibility for ourselves and for our relationships. Because of the vicissitudes of the human condition, sexual energy may be awakened before our emotions can handle it. Then our attitude toward sexual energy and its expression may be distorted. Relationships may be difficult, and we may even hesitate to give full consent to the goodness of our sexuality and creative potentialities.

When any emotion is felt to be dangerous, fear may repress that emotion into the unconscious, where it continues to express itself surreptitiously in physical illness or unhealthy forms of behavior. On the spiritual journey, we are invited to dismantle the false self. Part of that process is the dismantling of our repressive apparatus. As our trust in God grows, our defense mechanisms are no longer an essential means of survival. What has been repressed emerges from the secret hiding places of the unconscious. God allows this to happen because he is determined to give us another chance to integrate everything that is good into our ongoing development, including what we may have mistakenly perceived as not good.

The distortion of emotional development is seen in many persons on the Christian spiritual journey who suffer from the repression or rejection of their sexual feelings. Once such repression takes place, these people will have difficulty relating with genuine warmth to others. Sexual energy sustains the driving force of the motivation to serve other people with affection and warmth. People who have repressed their sexual feelings, or any other emotion for that matter, tend to repress their feelings across the board. This means that their capacity to relate to others in a supportive or affirming way is truncated. The fear that sexual energy may become uncontrollable tends to make them defensive; they avoid closeness with others because any form of expression of intimacy gives rise to an acute sense of danger. Later in life, the sexual energy may break through their defenses and present itself with twice as much force as in adolescence. The poignancy of a confrontation with overwhelming sexual feelings in midlife is obvious.

In early adulthood, God invites us to make a third consent: to accept the fact of our nonbeing and the diminutions of self that occur through illness, old age, and death. The passing of a friend or relative, or some accident, may invite us to reflect on our own death. Most cultures create means of pretending that death does not exist. When it happens, they cover it up as best they can with whatever cosmetics are available.

Acceptance of our nonbeing is directed not to the morbid side of death but rather to the consequences of dying: the letting go of everything we love in this world, whether persons, places, or things.

If we have suffered some great loss in early life such as the death of a parent, we may have an excessive fear of dying. Then we hesitate to make this consent. Moreover, if we have not made the previous consents, this one is more difficult.

The fourth consent is the consent to be transformed. We might think that everybody would be eager to make this one, but even the holiest people are inclined to say, "Let's not rush into this." The transforming union requires consent to the death of the false self, and the false self is the only self we know. Whatever its inconveniences, it is at least familiar. Some of us are more afraid of the death of the false self than of physical death.

These four consents are invitations to welcome life and death as God's gracious gifts and to appreciate the vocation of being a member of the human family in this marvelous universe with all its beauty and potentialities. Our consents, however, are not directed to the good things of life for their own sake or as ends in themselves. That would be idolatry. The emotional programs for happiness seek symbols of survival/security, affection/esteem, and power/control for the sake of the symbols themselves. Because of our fixations on particular programs for happiness, we treat survival/security, affection /esteem, and power/control symbols as absolutes, that is, as substitutes for God. Instead of being content with a reasonable amount of security, pleasure, and independence, we want to squeeze from these limited goods an absolute happiness that they cannot give. We then experience immediate disappointment and frustration.

This gradual training in consent is the school of divine love in which God invites us to accept the divine plan to share the divine life with us in a way that transcends all that the human imagination can foresee. We do not make these consents as ends in themselves, but rather to the will of God present in these things. We consent to God and to his will both in the enjoyment and in the surrender of his gifts. Each consent involves a kind of death. A child has to die to childhood in order to become an adolescent. An adolescent has to die to adolescence in order to enter the adult world. Most of us do not object in principle to growing up. In practice, however, we tend to hang on to our childish values, even as we grow up physically and intellectually. Consenting to God's will does not mean that we reject the values of any period of life as we pass through it; we simply leave behind its limitations.

Thus, the child's simplicity, innocence, enchantment with sense objects, and immediacy to sense experience are qualities that we should retain all through life. Only the tantrums and the ignorance of the child are left behind. Similarly, the spirit of adventure of the adolescent and the search for personal identity and relationship are values to be kept all through life; only the emotional turmoil of adolescence and the anxiety of establishing a personal identity are left behind as we become adults.

True asceticism is not the rejection of the world, but the acceptance of everything that is good, beautiful, and true. It is learning how to use our faculties and the good things of this world as God's gifts rather than expressions of selfishness. The basic ascesis is the appreciation of all that is good on each level of our developing humanity and the integration of the genuine values of each level into the next one. Integration is the unification of experience. As we perceive reality and relationship from new vantage points, we synthesize all that went before. This pattern continues beyond the mental egoic level of consciousness into further stages of human growth. The good things proper to the beginning of our spiritual journey have significant value, but we are asked to let them go as we move into more intimate relationships with God. While we do not reject the consolations of earlier times, we no longer depend on them or react to their withdrawal as we did in the beginning. We love God by loving all that he has made and everything that he does.

If we have not succeeded in making the consents proper to childhood, adolescence, and young adulthood, we may be invited to do so in later life under the inspiration of grace. God often invites us to rethink the judgments we made in childhood and adolescence, or in the early years of our conversion, that amounted to a rejection of the goodness of his gifts. He invites us to take another look at our hesitations and to realize that our rigid attitudes were based on our inability to handle events and relationships that were emotionally traumatic. Now he asks us to accept the legitimate pleasures of life, the value of friendship, the exercise of our talents, the loveliness of nature, the beauty of art, the enjoyment of both activity and rest. God is a tremendous supporter of creation, especially of all living beings. Jesus emphasized this when he said, "I came that they might have life and have it to the full" (John 10:10). The abundant life is divine union, which includes the capacity to use all things as stepping stones to God rather than as ends in themselves. To access this state, however, requires the willingness to negotiate the first three consents.

By consenting to God's creation, to our basic goodness as human beings, and to the letting go of what we love in this world, we are brought to the final surrender, which is to allow the false self to die and the true self to emerge. The true self might be described as our participation in the divine life manifesting in our uniqueness. God has more than one way of bringing us to this point. It can happen early in adult life, but if it does not, the ongoing stages of natural life may contribute to bringing it about. In the midlife crisis, even very successful people wonder whether they have accomplished anything. Later we experience physical decline, illness, and the infirmities of old age. What happens in the process of dying may be God's way of correcting all the mistakes we made and all the opportunities we missed during the earlier part of our lives. It may also provide the greatest chance of all to consent to God's gift of ourselves.

9

Bernie

The story of Brother Bernie O'Shea exemplifies what consent to the basic goodness of our own being and nature might look like in actual practice. Bernie entered the monastery at seventeen immediately after finishing high school. He was a warm, affectionate, loving young man who enjoyed close relationships. At the time, the members of the Trappist order, because of the strict rule of silence, lived like hermits in community. Whether Bernie fully realized what this meant before he entered, I do not know, but in he came with his broad smile, exuberance, and bouncing step. He immediately tried to make friends with all the other novices. Since he could only use sign language to communicate, he learned all two hundred signs in one day. He then pressed into service every available occasion to relate.

One of the best opportunities came when someone held the door for him so that he could pass from the novitiate into the cloister. Bernie would watch for this opportunity so as to be able to make the sign for "thank you." To make this sign, we brought the fingertips of our right hands to our lips and kissed them, but we were not supposed to make any noise. When anyone opened the door for him, Bernie was delighted. Like a baseball pitcher winding up to deliver a fast ball, he would rotate his right arm, bring his fingers to his lips with a great flourish and a big smack, and look into your eyes with his broadest possible smile. It was a marvelous encounter the first time, but after three or four times in one day, I, for one, had a strong inclination to go in the opposite direction when I saw him coming.

The superiors were aware that Bernie was socially inclined and decided he would do better as a lay brother. In that vocation he could find more opportunities for practical services and hence more opportunities for signs, and even an occasional spoken word if the nature of the work required it. The superiors decided that cooking would be a good job for him. This was not an easy assignment for Bernie. For him to learn to cook meant copying page after page of recipes and writing all kinds of accessory instructions to himself in the margins.

When the community prepared to move from Valley Falls, Rhode Island, to a dairy farm in Spencer, Massachusetts, Bernie was sent to cook for the two monks who were in charge of converting the cow barns into a monastery. This was Bernie's first opportunity since joining the order to relate to people outside the cloister. His innate friendliness was now given a little scope.

After the disastrous fire in March 1950 that virtually destroyed the old monastery in Rhode Island, the abbot sent me to Spencer to replace the priest in charge, who was now needed to renovate an abandoned camp for immediate occupancy by the community back home. I arrived on the premises in full monastic fervor, having been ordained a priest just a year before.

The former owner of the farm and his family were still living on the property. Bernie had already made friends with his wife. They enjoyed swapping recipes, and they both had a flare for music and loved decorative objects. One day while I was out for a walk, they got together and put some curtains in the windows, rugs on the floor, and a few knickknacks on the window sills. When I walked in, I was shocked. The Trappists at that time were noted for their simplicity of lifestyle. We used to sit on benches. There was no such thing at the old monastery as a chair with a back, a rug on the floor, or curtains at the windows. I said to myself, "This is contrary to the Trappist spirit!" I felt it was my duty as the one in charge to uphold the rule. Accordingly, a few days later when Bernie went out for a walk, I removed all the curtains, rugs, and knickknacks. When he came back and saw the devastation, his heart must have been broken, but he put up with the decision, of course, because I was in charge. Fortunately for him, he was transferred back to Rhode Island shortly afterward and escaped from my austere regime.

There was a tendency in the Trappist tradition that we had inherited to disapprove of any kind of enjoyment. Indulging in simple pleasures was considered a form of falling back into the ways of the world. Bernie could not understand what was wrong about enjoying art, music, flowers, sunsets, and people. When a new monastery was started in Colorado in the late 1950s, the abbot sent Bernie there to cook for those who were constructing it. When Bernie arrived in the beautiful Roaring Fork Valley with his big stack of cookbooks, he immediately fell in love with the mountains, the clouds, the nights full of stars, and springtime in the Rockies. Nobody ever loved that mountain valley as Bernie did. The flowers fascinated him. He could become ecstatic over a daisy. Some people used to think his reaction was a put-on. It was not! Later, when I was sent to Snowmass, he used to say to me, "God speaks to me through the flowers. Is there anything wrong with that?" I had to say, "I guess there is nothing wrong with that," but I really did not agree. I thought that his priorities were in disarray and that he should be more interested in prayer, spiritual reading, and penitential practices.

Actually Bernie was a faithful reader of the gospels, but he had little interest in reading other things. He often said that a few sentences from the gospel were enough for him. Then he liked to go out into the woods or onto a mountainside and watch the clouds, the flowers, the elk, the porcupines, and the eagles if he could spot one.

Bernie's social proclivities were severely curtailed by our strict rule of silence. He could not understand what was wrong with socializing or having an occasional party, but in those days we rarely had a feast. I can remember when it was a startling innovation to sing a few carols on Christmas day. Later our abbot, who was ahead of his time, allowed ice cream on certain great feasts, but rarely and in the silence of the refectory.

Bernie often expressed deep self-doubts because he realized the order had different ideas from his about how to be a monk. He felt that the supreme value of monastic life was the community and that loving the brothers and serving them was the best way to express this value. He could not understand the idea of hermits in community. He approved of solitude, but he thought that silence was overdone. He felt there should be more opportunities for communication. He accepted the status quo, however, and continued to cook and work hard to please the community. After three and a half years in Snowmass, I was elected abbot of the motherhouse and returned to Spencer.

Following the Second Vatican Council, religious orders were urged to review their respective observances in the light of modern conditions and the charism of their founders. Changes in the Trappist order began to take place rapidly. The rule of silence was modified, and the local superior was given discretionary powers with regard to many rules that up to then had been regarded as inviolable. In this way events like celebrations or hikes could be permitted.

Bernie experienced these changes as an affirmation of his own monastic orientation. For many years he had thought he was the only one in the order who was crazy. Now it seemed that the order was beginning to move in the direction he thought it should have espoused in the first place. This encouraged him to follow still more his attraction to serve the community and to show love in every possible way. He developed his service into an art. If genius is the art of taking pains, Bernie was a genius. He enlarged his benign sphere of influence beyond the kitchen. Not only was he concerned that the brothers and the guests had the right food, but also that they had enough blankets and clothes; that they saw a herd of elk when one was out there; and that, if they were visitors, they had the chance to see the local sights. He sponsored hikes into the mountains and the celebration of birthdays, homecomings, and anniversaries.

A party in those days consisted of a chance to chat and to enjoy a few goodies, especially ice cream. One of Bernie's favorite pranks at parties was to tease the more austere members of the community. He would make himself a bowl of ice cream beginning with four or five scoops of chocolate or vanilla. On top of that he would pour a generous helping of hot fudge sauce. On top of that would go an enormous portion of whipped cream, and finally a fistful of pecans to top it off. Then he would sit down in the presence of any number of hard-nosed ascetics and eat this concoction, smacking his lips in delight. His philosophy was, "If you are going to indulge in some legitimate pleasure, why not enjoy it?" He could not figure out why monks experience guilt feelings whenever they encounter some innocent pleasure.

In a western household, the kitchen is the center of the home, the place where everybody usually enters and leaves. This was Bernie's kingdom. From there he ruled the roost. He was the abbot's right-hand man, whether by choice or circumstance. He enjoyed complete freedom to take an interest in visitors to the monastery. He showed so much interest, in fact, that people who met him once rarely forgot him. He would even take vicarious pleasure in what the guests ate in restaurants in Aspen. If they stayed overnight in the monastery, he was concerned that they have a good breakfast. When my brother visited, he was impressed that Bernie insisted on serving him eggs and bacon, a treat the community was not permitted.

I came regularly to Snowmass in those days as the official visitor on behalf of the order, to encourage and check out the community. The visitor interviewed the members of the community for most of the day, listening to their opinions about the way the observances were going and to the difficulties they might be experiencing. Bernie perceived that this might be a fatiguing occupation, so he used to bring me a cup of tea and, of course, a few cookies to go along with it. Such things as coffee breaks were still unheard of, and I was hesitant at first about this favor, but he took such pleasure in doing this service that I could not say no. Bernie challenged us to accept his special acts of kindness by making us feel as if we were doing him a favor.

At a certain point in the process of renewal, the lay brothers' vocation was integrated with that of the choir monks, to the great dissatisfaction of many lay brothers, including Bernie. He reflected, however, that in a small community everybody has to pitch in. Although he had no inclination to join the choir, he learned how to play the organ in order to offer the gift of his presence to the common prayer. He loved every kind of music. When he accompanied the chant, he had a tendency—such was his taste—to pull out the tremolo. To someone trained in the purity of Gregorian chant, this was not exactly the last word in sacred music. But clearly his efforts were proof of his determination to serve the needs of the community.

Over the years I kept coming back for visits and could see that Bernie was growing in maturity as well as in loving kindness. He was less obtrusive in pushing his charitable intentions on others; at the same time he always seemed to be on hand when you needed something.

On one occasion, the local abbot attended a workshop and was convinced that the community would benefit from a macrobiotic diet. By dint of dogged perseverance, Bernie was at this time one of the best cooks in the order. When the community agreed to this new diet as an experiment, Bernie went along with it although it meant the disruption of all his carefully worked out and annotated recipes. All the goodies he loved to prepare and to eat were ruled out by this diet. Carrot juice, uncooked vegetables, and sugarless desserts, all totally foreign to his taste, were the order of the day. Fortunately for him, everyone starting getting sick, including the abbot. Gradually the health food diet was modified and eventually laid to rest.

Every now and then, the community had what they called an evaluation meeting. The monks could bring up matters of concern with regard to the community. On one occasion the question was raised, "Would it be all right to see a movie once in a while, or some exceptional program on TV?" Each monk, as was customary, gave his opinion. Some expressed concern that this might bring the spirit of the world into the monastery. "It is not our vocation," they said. When everyone had given his opinion, Bernie, who had originally brought up the idea, said, "What if all the people watching TV at this very moment are holier than we are?" No one was able to answer that question, and so a television set was brought in to show an occasional video. I suspect that that was what everyone wanted to do anyway. Bernie was just more honest and outspoken.

Although the occasions were rare, Bernie loved to go to Aspen and window-shop. When he heard people say, "Aspen is sin city, the Babylon of the West, the cocaine capital of America," he would defend it, saying, "I find God in Aspen." Because he had a special love for *National Geographic* specials, the abbot occasionally allowed him to drop into the local rectory when he was in town to view a documentary about whales or other nature subjects.

When I resigned as abbot of Spencer in the fall of 1981, the community in Snowmass graciously invited me to come there to live. Everyone welcomed me warmly, but I could see that Bernie's mind was working overtime. His reflections seemed to run along these lines: "This guy has been abbot of a big monastery and has been in the service of the order for twenty years. Now he is living in this insignificant little community. He must miss the big one that he left behind and all the brothers there. He needs special consideration." Instead of treating me like everybody else, he went out of his way to find out what food I liked and what food I could not eat, in addition to all his other ever-increasing activities. I remember reflecting, "This must be the way God is!" When someone treats you in such a way that it makes you think of God, that person clearly is a sacrament of God's presence.

During my first Thanksgiving celebration at Snowmass, Bernie, as was his wont, was banging on the piano and happened to play a melody that I was especially fond of. I wanted to ask him to put it on a cassette so that I could listen to it from time to time, but there was so much going on at the party that I was not able to mention my request to him.

A few weeks later, the abbot and I were attending a meeting of superiors at another monastery. While we were there, the abbot had a phone call notifying him that Bernie had dropped dead on the street in Aspen. He had gone to the dentist and was on his way to take my clerical suit to the cleaners. A final stop at the local rectory to see a video about whales had been scheduled, but he had had a massive heart attack and died instantly.

The abbot was completely broken up by the news. He flew back at once, asking me to stay to represent him at the meeting. Two days later I flew back and landed at the airport in Aspen. It was a glorious winter day and Colorado was at its best—bright blue sky, a few white clouds, snow, green fir trees, and the air as clear as crystal. I could not help thinking, "This valley is celebrating! It belongs to Bernie because he loved it so much."

When we got into the car, the brother who picked me up said, "Would you like to hear Bernie's voice again?" I said, "What do you mean? How can I hear his voice again?" He replied, "A few days before Bernie died, we made an audio cassette together for my brother's twenty-fifth wedding anniversary." Characteristically, Bernie had wanted to provide a little surprise for one of the monks' relatives with whom he had made friends. Bernie and this brother had produced a skit in which Bernie played the role of a piano player in a night club in Aspen. The other brother played the role of an announcer for the local radio station who was interviewing him. I said, "By all means, turn it on!"

The brother turned on the cassette player. What do you think came out? The piece that Bernie was playing on the piano was the tune I had wanted him to put on a cassette for me. I thought to myself, "My God, Bernie, you really are thoughtful! Here you are in glory and you are thinking of this trifling request of mine!" The coincidence was so typical of him that it was absolutely impossible for me to interpret it in any other way.

I never knew anyone who resembled sunshine more than this man. No one ever loved life so genuinely and consented to its goodness so unreservedly. Yet right away, at God's request, he dropped everything. That is true detachment—accepting everything that God wants us to accept and letting go of everything that God wants us to let go of, at a moment's notice.

10

Anthony as a Paradigm of the Spiritual Journey

Saint Anthony of Egypt, the fourth-century father of Christian monasticism, is one of the few holy people whose inner spiritual journey we know in considerable detail. His biography provides a paradigm for dismantling the false self by means of both active confrontation and passive purification. Bernie, of course, exemplifies the positive way of dismantling the false self by practicing unconditional love: selfishness cannot survive in the climate of continuous self-giving. A combination of the two ways may be the most practical response to the human condition.

In the preceding chapters, we have been looking at the dynamics involved in the development of the false self and at how the false self interferes with the proper exercise of our relationships with God, ourselves, and others. Dismantling it often feels like interior warfare—and in fact, it is! Anthony of Egypt, the champion of the ascetic life, is the perfect paradigm for this approach to the spiritual journey. By taking this inward path, he too reached perfect love, at which point he manifested the lively concern for the needs of others that Bernie manifested and practiced.

These two paths should not be presented in opposition to each other. Both are needed for a balanced spiritual development. Anthony is especially helpful in that he exemplifies the heart of the Christian journey, whether the emphasis is placed on its positive or negative aspects: namely, the struggle with unconscious motivation. The cross that Jesus invites each of us to carry is precisely the emotional wounds that we bring with us from early childhood, together with the coping mechanisms we developed to deal with them. Although original sin is not the result of personal wrongdoing on our part, it causes a pervasive feeling of alienation from God, from other people, and from our true selves.

The term *original sin* is a way of describing the universal experience of coming to full reflective self-consciousness without the certitude of personal union with God. This gives rise to our intimate sense of incompletion, dividedness, isolation, and guilt. The cultural consequences of these alienations are instilled in us from earliest childhood and passed on from one generation to the next. The urgent need to escape from the profound insecurity of this situation, when unchecked, gives rise to insatiable desires for pleasure, possessions, and power. On the social level, it gives rise to violence, war, and institutional injustice.

The particular consequences of original sin include all the self-serving habits that have been woven into our personalities from the time we were conceived; all the harm that other people have done to us knowingly or unknowingly at an age when we could not defend ourselves; and the methods we acquired, many of them now unconscious, to ward off the pain of unbearable situations. This constellation of prerational reactions is the foundation of the false self. The false self develops in opposition to the true self. Its center of gravity is the self as separate from God and others, and hence turned in on itself.

In Anthony's time, demons were familiar figures in the popular culture both within and without the Christian community. Thus, it is not surprising that Anthony's biographer, Saint Athanasius, Bishop of Alexandria, describes Anthony's ascetical life as a series of combats with Satan.[1] In fact, spiritual combat was a vivid theme for the early Church—and a recent literal memory.

Prior to the Edict of Milan in 313, which established peace between the Roman Empire and the Christian Church, the great symbol of Christian perfection was fidelity to the gospel in the face of persecution. During the first three centuries, Christians lived with the daily prospect of being thrown to the lions, sent to the mines, or ostracized and banned from any kind of public career. The Edict of Milan was an event of enormous significance for this persecuted Church whose membership was composed largely of slaves and the poor. Once martyrdom was no longer a daily prospect, fervent Christians started looking for a lifestyle that would express a similar dedication to Christ.

When Athanasius wrote *The Life of Saint Anthony* in the mid-fourth century, a few years after the death of Anthony, he affirmed that the same Spirit who prompted the generosity of the martyrs was still present in the Church and calling people to a new expression of dedication to Christ. Athanasius coined the term "the daily martyrdom of conscience" for the practice of asceticism that Anthony had inaugurated in the desert. The generosity of seeking God day after day by means of asceticism was compared to the generosity of laying down one's life in the arena. And Athanasius dared to say, "They are equal." Asceticism thus became the ideal way to lead a fervent Christian life in times of peace.

Anthony was born about 251 in a little town in lower Egypt. His well-to-do parents owned a fertile farm of about two hundred acres. We are told that Anthony was a fair-haired boy who ate what was put before him and was obedient to his parents. Tragedy hit this happy home, although we are not told exactly what happened. Perhaps

Anthony's parents were killed in a chariot accident. In any event, the young man of eighteen was left in charge of the estate and of his younger sister.

One day, while thinking of how the apostles had given up everything in order to follow Christ, Anthony happened to go into the local church. The gospel text being proclaimed (Matt. 19:21–23) went right to his heart: "If you seek perfection, go, sell your possessions, and give to the poor. You will then have treasure in heaven. Afterward come back and follow me." (This is the same text that later inspired the conversion of Saint Francis of Assisi.) Anthony immediately sold everything he had, keeping back just a little to take care of his sister. Although this was surely a prudent judgment, God had other plans. A few weeks later Anthony entered the church again, and this time he heard the text, "Stop worrying, then, over questions like, 'What are we to eat, or what are we to drink, or what are we to wear?'" (Matt. 6:31). Cut to the quick, he gave away the meager savings he had reserved to take care of his sister and placed her with a group of devout women.

Anthony was now free to pursue his attraction for asceticism. There was no organized form of religious life at that time, so he sought out the two chief benefits of the common life, namely, the support of good example and the advice of those who had been on the spiritual journey for a long time. Under this tutelage, he soon began to experience the springtime of the spiritual life, the first fruits of his generosity. Athanasius's text sums up Anthony's zeal in practicing the virtues:

> He observed the graciousness of one, the earnestness in prayer of another; he studied the even temper of one and the kindheartedness of another. He fixed his attention on the vigils kept by one and on the studies pursued by another. He admired one for his patient

endurance, another for his fasting and sleeping on the ground. He watched closely one man's meekness and the forbearance by another. And in one and all alike he marked especially their devotion to Christ and the love that they had for one another. (*The Life of St. Anthony*, No. 4, 21)

Notice the bond that unites the members of the group amid their diversity of gifts: the love of Christ and their love for one another. The deeper the unity, the more pluralism a community can absorb. The variety of viewpoints and gifts are experienced not as threats to one's own practice and views, but as enrichments.

Now comes the statement that intones the basic theme of the first stages of Anthony's journey, which Athanasius presents as an ever-increasing struggle with the powers of evil:

The devil, the hater and envier of good, could not bear to see such resolution in the young man, but set about employing his customary tactics against him. (*The Life of St. Anthony*, No. 5, 22)

The term "customary tactics" suggests a program of testing neophytes on the spiritual journey to see what their weak points are, and then of pressing hard on those weaknesses in order to persuade them to give up the spiritual journey and return to their former occupations. In other words, the envier of all that is good tempts us to give up following Christ and to go back to cultivating the false self.

Anthony at the time had already logged several months of intense asceticism, living in extreme privation. As a modern equivalent, we might picture him living at the edge of town in a tiny shack overlooking the local garbage dump. The springtime of Anthony's journey had passed; interior consolation had dried up, and he was famished from fasting. Suddenly his imagination was stirred. The demon began to remind him of the pleasures he had enjoyed in his former lifestyle.

The first thing that came into his mind was the memory of his property. He saw once again the fertile land with the flowing waters of the Nile glistening in the setting sun. Everything was so peaceful. Stringed instruments played soft music in the distance. Anthony could smell the delicious perfume of flowers like hyacinth or wisteria. Sight, smell, taste, touch, and sound all combined in his imagination and memory to awaken an immense nostalgia for that beautiful property, especially on those long, lovely summer evenings. Then a voice close to his ear seemed to whisper, "Anthony, how could you leave such a gorgeous property? It's still there. It's not too late. If you leave right away, you can easily get it back!"

The spiritual entity called the devil could well be a great stage and screen producer. Cecil B. deMille was amateurish by comparison. By stirring up the senses and choosing just the right images, the devil evokes the most tender memories and the most poignant feelings in order to create the maximum impression. His purpose: to weaken one's resolve to continue the spiritual journey.

But Anthony was unmoved in his resolve. The devil's next temptation conjured up memories of intimacy with former friends and relatives. In the ascetic life, it was no longer appropriate to have any contact with them. In fact, Anthony's friends must have heard of his new lifestyle and probably did not want to go anywhere near him. The devil reminded Anthony, "No longer will you be able to see your dear little sister. . . No more affectionate embraces, no more family gatherings, no more birthday parties." The sweetest memories of family and friends came floating down the stream of his consciousness. But Anthony remained firm.

Anthony's next temptation was calculated to awaken greed for money. As we saw, Anthony had given away all his possessions for the love of Christ, even the meager funds he had thought of using to provide for his sister. Now as he sat in his poverty-stricken shack, the desire for money passed before his mind's eye. The devil suggested all the wonderful things he could use it for: pleasures, travel, studies, high finance, perhaps even investments to amass funds to give to the poor! But Anthony paid no attention to the endless procession of possibilities.

His next temptation appealed to the desire for power. This young man who had never known power over anyone began to feel the attraction to control the other ascetics. A mysterious and insidious voice whispered, "Anthony, if only you had stayed where you were, you could have had a fine job at the local fertilizer plant. It's not too late! With your talents, you could be a junior executive in no time! Perhaps even a senior executive! And in a little while you would become the president of the company! Then you could buy up all the fertilizer plants in Egypt!" Notice how this kind of temptation builds up and becomes more and more grandiose. But Anthony was prompt in letting go of each suggestion.

Next came the attraction to become famous. This form of vanity was so incongruous, given the kind of life that Anthony had chosen, that it made no impression on him at all.

His imagination and memory were then subtly directed to the amenities of life: sports, hi-fi's, movies, holidays, good housing, all the comforts of life. All that was most charming and entrancing in his early life passed in review. These memories were in sharp contrast to his tin-can shack and unobstructed view of the dump. He winced at the contrast but did not entertain these pleasurable thoughts.

Next came the memory of the pleasures of food and drink. This young man from a well-fed household had been fasting for months on one meal a day of simple vegetables, often of just bread and water. Thoughts of the good old days were dangled before his mind's eye. Perhaps he recalled those delicious crocodile burgers by the Nile. The bottom line to all these impressions was always the same: "Anthony, do not delay! You must leave. Do not think twice about it. Go back to your luxurious property! Go back to your career! Go back to your friends! Go back to those sumptuous meals!"

These worldly temptations that kept pounding him were not outside him, but inside him. That is what made them so disconcerting and confusing. What was his method of resistance? Faith, determination, and incessant prayer. Anthony was resolved not to give up the spiritual journey. This is his timeless message to those on the journey: never stop waiting for God, never stop trusting in God, never stop praying to God.

The devil was nonplussed by Anthony's steadfast resolution. He suspected that Anthony, by escaping unharmed from these temptations, might undermine his malignant influence over the local population. Though the positive attraction to return to the pleasant things of the world had failed, the demon had another card up his sleeve: to weaken Anthony's resolution to persevere in the spiritual journey by attracting him to leave under the pretext of a greater good. Generous followers of Christ cannot normally be tempted by the raw attraction of evil, nor will they exchange the spiritual journey for respectable mediocrity. The suggestion of a greater good is the only -way to catch them.

The voice of the devil now challenged Anthony's resolution with the following considerations. "Anthony, what have you done? You have put your little sister in that community of austere, gloomy, horse-faced women! Despite their pretensions of piety, they are a bunch of old witches. They never smile. They won't let her play with her doll. They beat her whenever she commits the slightest fault. She's crying her heart out! You must leave instantly and rescue her!"

This kind of temptation is a dirty trick if there ever was one. Sometimes those we love raise a similar problem of conscience. There was a novice in my monastery whose mother used to write regularly saying, "If you do not come home, I will commit suicide!" Imagine getting that message on a cold, dark, damp fast day. The monk stayed and his mother continued to go on living.

I had a grandma who doted on me because I was named after my deceased grandfather whom she adored. We used to do many things together. After my conversion from worldly objectives to the values of the gospel, she could not understand my increasing interest in spiritual things. When I told her that I intended to enter a cloistered Trappist monastery, it was just the end. She had been brought up in a tradition that associated monks with lurid tales about finding the skulls of infants in underground passages between adjoining monasteries of men and women. Her idea of a monk was someone in the last stages of degeneracy.

In her last illness, Grandma was bedridden in an apartment in New York, attended by nurses around the clock. One day I received a letter from her which read, "Dearest Grandson, I'm lying in my bed and I miss you terribly. I still hope you will come home. Over and over I say to my nurse, 'If my grandson won't come home, won't you please throw me out of the window!'"

My first reaction was, "How can I justify causing so much suffering to someone who loves me so much?" This kind of trial tests our vocation to the roots and sifts our motives. If we came to the monastery because we wanted to be a farmer, a liturgist, or a country dweller, we would not last very long.

Here are a few contemporary scenarios for this subtle kind of temptation. The bottom line is always the same one: drop your commitment to the spiritual journey in favor of a greater good. There follows the voice of the tempter:

"Dear Soul, you were studying to be a doctor and doing so well. Doctors are badly needed. Why not return to your career? You could serve people so much more generously . . ."

"Dear Friend, your mother and father are at each other's throats again. You are the only one who was ever able to bring peace to the home. If you leave now, you can make everything peaceful again . . ."

"Dearest One, your old flame is sitting in a furnished room with the tears streaming down her cheeks. Her heart is breaking. How can you do this to her?" Actually she has met a wonderful guy, has never been happier, and has not given you a second thought, but the devil never suggests another possible side to the story. He builds up a huge smokescreen of arguments to support his thesis. We are treated to a production that is compelling, absorbing, but completely unreal.

When the devil was not able to persuade Anthony to return to his former way of life, he tried to insinuate a negative attitude toward the ascetic life that Anthony had embraced. His first ploy was to suggest weakness of the body and the rigors of asceticism. "Anthony, how long do you expect to survive like this? You will soon be ill. You may die!" He reminded Anthony of the long journey still ahead and of how endless time can seem in adverse circumstances. "How can you keep up this attack against the false self month after month, year after year?"

Finally, the devil pointed to the great labor of practicing virtue and dismantling the emotional programs of happiness. "How can you give up your desire to control things and other people? You are a superior person!" Or again, "Why give up your desire for security? You've earned it!" And as a final shot, "You entered on this path much too young. You'll never make it as a lifelong celibate!"

Every temptation is tailor-made to fit one's personal history and particular vulnerability. The rigor of virtue, the duration of time, and the great labor of practicing virtue are temptations that arise in various forms and degrees of intensity. One form is the feeling of incompatibility with one's spouse, family, or the members of one's community. When it came time for me to make a final commitment to the Trappist order, I had to face the searching question, "How am I going to live for the next fifty or sixty years with this person whose fidelity to prayer makes me unbearably envious?"

To each of his temptations Anthony gave the same basic response: determination to persevere in the spiritual journey, trust that God would give him the grace to do so, and incessant prayer. Each of these three dispositions is an exercise of faith, hope, and love.

11

The Night of Sense

Freedom from the False Self

A nthony's temptations to abandon the spiritual journey, as we saw, were of two kinds. One was the positive attraction to things he had enjoyed in his former lifestyle. The other was the feeling of aversion for the ascetical life that he had embraced. Why did he experience such strong and repeated temptations to return to the life he had so vigorously renounced when he initially committed himself to the spiritual journey?

The answer is that Anthony's emotional programs for happiness were still present on the unconscious level; it was to the hidden contents of Anthony's unconscious that the devil kept appealing. To decide consciously to follow the values of the gospel is only the first step in our commitment to Christ. The *values in the unconscious* must then be confronted. When the springtime of the spiritual journey subsides, the old temptations surface once again with the same or more force than before our conversion.

The spiritual journey is characterized by the ever-increasing knowledge of our mixed motivations, the dark sides of our personalities, and the emotional traumas of early childhood. Nothing is more helpful to reduce pride than the actual experience of self-knowledge. If we are discouraged by it, we have misunderstood its meaning.

What is our experience when we start to dismantle the false self and refuse to act out of our emotional programs? God seems to come closer. Since God is always present, it might be better to say he turns up the voltage in our interior world. A room that is well appointed and cleaned every day looks pretty clean. We are happy to sit in it. If, however, fifty ten-thousand-watt bulbs are turned on and the floor is put under a magnifying glass, the whole room would be crawling with little creatures. We would leave as fast as possible.

God responds to our generosity as if saying, "This person is serious about the spiritual journey. Let's go to work and clean out the junk." God turns up the voltage and, as a consequence, our inner world begins to crawl, so to speak; the damage that our emotional programs for happiness are doing to us and to our relationships becomes apparent. From this perspective our good deeds look like piles of dirty dishrags.

Saint John of the Cross, the sixteenth-century Spanish mystic, has distinguished this difficult period more articulately than any other spiritual writer. He calls it the night of sense. The first sign of the presence of this night is a generalized aridity in both prayer and daily life. This dryness or diminution of satisfaction in our relationships with God is the direct effect of an increase of faith and the beginning of contemplative prayer. God is beaming an increase of divine light into our inner world, but we do not have the receptive apparatus to properly interpret the experience. It feels like a great loss. What is lost? The free and easy exchanges that we had previously enjoyed with God as a result of fruitful reflection on the scriptures, reception of the sacraments, prayer, and the service of others. When we pick up the scriptures, it is an effort to sit still with the text for the time that we had agreed upon. Spiritual reading is like reading a telephone book. As sensible grace begins to fade, the lack of any feeling of benefit in spiritual exercises increases. At the same time, we do not find satisfaction in worldly things. The growth of faith, under the influence of what theology calls the gift of knowledge, one of the seven gifts of the Holy Spirit, produces this lack of satisfaction, both in things relating to God and in the emotional programs in which we had placed a heavy investment. The Holy Spirit infuses into our minds the insight that God alone can satisfy our boundless longing for happiness. This positive experience is not a dissatisfaction with anything—pleasure, power, or security. It springs from the realization that no created thing can bring us unlimited satisfaction. In the light of this intuition, we know that all the gratifications we were seeking when we were motivated by our emotional programs cannot possibly bring us happiness. This creates a period of mourning, during which all the things that we had counted on to bring us happiness are slowly relativized.

According to John of the Cross, the second sign of this growth in the spiritual journey is manifested by the fear that we are going backwards and that through some personal fault or failure we have offended God. Since there is no felt affirmation coming from grace, we can get into quite a stew. Some people mistakenly think it is the end of their relationships with God. This is not true. What has ended is their overdependence on the senses and reasoning in order to pray. God is offering them a more intimate relationship; if they would not reflect on their anxious feelings, they would begin to perceive it. In this state we are like a baby being weaned from the breast. Infants are generally opposed to this development, but once they learn to accept the situation, they enjoy the more nourishing food of meat and potatoes. It is part of growing up. The night of sense is a period of weaning from the consolations that characterized the beginning of our relationships with God. The solid nourishment of pure faith is an acquired taste, like solid food for the weaned child.

The third sign of the night of sense identified by John of the Cross is the inability or disinclination to practice discursive meditation. Discursive meditation, in which one ponders the teaching and example of Jesus, is generally prescribed as a preliminary step to contemplative prayer. Without the inclination to meditate discursively, the mind wanders far and wide. The will finds no benefit or pleasure in particular acts of love, praise, petition, or any other response to God's gifts. Still, we desire to be alone with God, even though he seems to be a million miles away and to have lost interest in us.

John of the Cross states that all three signs should be present together in discerning the night of sense. If only one and not the others is present, there could be some pathology such as a depression.

The night of sense, John of the Cross asserts, happens "fairly soon" to those who commit themselves to the spiritual journey. By the term *night* John of the Cross means the darkening of the usual ways in which we relate to God, whether through reflection or through the experience of the senses. Our ordinary ways of relating to God are being changed to ways that we do not know. This pulls the rug out from under our plans and strategies for the spiritual journey. We learn that the journey is a path that cannot be mapped out in advance. God helps us to disidentify from our preconceived ideas by enlightening us from within by the contemplative gifts of the Spirit. Through the infusion of his light and the assurance of his love, he lets us in on our weaknesses and deficiencies—not to overwhelm us with discouragement, but to encourage us to entrust ourselves completely to his infinite mercy.

12

Special Trials in the Night of Sense

When the night of sense is prolonged, three particular trials may arise. Although they make this transitional period more difficult, they also accelerate its progress and enable us, once and for all, to put to rest the predominating influence and motivation of the false self These temptations do not occur in everyone, nor do all three usually occur in the same person. They are sure signs that we are in the night of sense.

Here is how John of the Cross describes the first trial:

> For to some the angel of Satan presents himself—namely, the spirit of fornication—that he may buffet their senses with abominable and violent temptations, and trouble their spirits with vile considerations and representations which are most visible to the imagination, which things at times are a greater affliction to them than death. (*Dark Night of the Soul*, Ch. 14, no. 1)

Anthony's experience of this temptation is thoroughly described by Athanasius. We are told that immediately after he had resisted the positive and negative temptations to return to his former lifestyle, the devil pulled this trick out of his bag. He began by lobbing pornographic images into Anthony's imagination, somewhat the way an invading army lobs mortars into a city to soften up the opposition before the troops move in. The next salvo involved the stirring up of sexual feelings. This trial apparently went on for some weeks or months. The text says that the struggle between Anthony and the demon was so intense that his colleagues could sense the battle that was going on.

When vivid temptations of this kind continue for a long time, our conscience may become confused as to whether it has consented or not. We think, "If I am really rejecting them, why do they keep coming back?" As obsessive thoughts and emotions keep returning, the full force of the sexual energy comes into focus. Since Anthony had led a withdrawn life in early childhood, he was probably not aware of its power. He had made a commitment to celibacy in order to channel his whole strength into the single-hearted pursuit of the spiritual journey. He needed to confront and accept the full force of his sexual energy in order to allow the Spirit to transmute it into zeal for the service of God and of his future disciples.

After weeks and perhaps months of constant struggling with these temptations, Anthony experienced the devil's final assault. It might be verbalized as follows: "Anthony, you have done your very best, but your best efforts are evidently not working at all. You might as well give in." Anthony responded with anger and grief, certain signs that his will was not consenting.

Anthony acted on the energy aroused by his anger in a practical way. He introduced into his mind's eye a vivid image of the fires of hell. This strategy was not designed to stir up the emotion of fear, which is counterproductive in temptations to sexual misconduct. The body responds to the feeling of fear by pouring chemicals into the blood stream and concentrating the flow of blood in the abdomen in order to prepare the body to fight or run away. Anthony's strategy was to introduce a lively image of material fire on the same level as his urgent attractions to sexual pleasure. By putting the image of material fire and its pain into his imagination, he was able to put out the fire of lust.

When Anthony came through this temptation unscathed, the devil, we are told, immediately changed his tactics. Fawning and saying Anthony was not like other people who are all easy prey to temptation, he tried to persuade Anthony to take personal credit for his victory over sensuality, and thus fall into spiritual pride. Anthony's response was, and I paraphrase, "To hell with you! . . ." "This," Athanasius says, "was Anthony's first victory over Satan."

Thus, in addition to refusing to consent to the spirit of fornication, Anthony refused to consent to the more subtle gratification of victory over his temptations. The pride of innocence is one of the most dangerous forms of pride. It attributes to oneself what only the grace of God can enable one to do. The risk at this point in the spiritual journey is that freedom from personal sin and ease in the practice of virtue may go to one's head.

The night of sense reveals the full extent of the selfishness of which we are capable. Humility is the fruit of the bittersweet experience of this intimate kind of self-knowledge. It is the peaceful acknowledgment of our faults without the reactions of blame, shame, anger, or discouragement. Self-recriminations are neurotic. They are the voice of wounded pride saying, "You've done it again, you dumb so-and-so! You always foul things up. You don't measure up to my (fantastic) standards of perfection." Humility is the balance between the truth about weakness and confidence in the infinite mercy of God.

John of the Cross describes a second temptation in the night of sense:

> At other times in this night there is added to these things the spirit of blasphemy, which roams abroad, setting in the path of all the conceptions and thoughts of the soul intolerable blasphemies.

These it sometimes suggests to the imagination with such violence that the soul almost utters them, which is a grave torment to it. (*Dark Night of the Soul*, Ch. 14, no. 2)

Some persons who experience this trial conclude that they are failing God and that their former friendship is at an end. Their anxiety is thus intensified.

The sense of helplessness in the face of raw anger can occur in any lifestyle. When I emerged from the novitiate into the professed house, I was given the chore of assisting the sacristan in preparing the vestments for the celebration of the Eucharist. Because I wanted to spend all my free time in prayer, I used to rush in from work, wash up, and go directly to church. The sacristan sometimes intercepted me along the way with a sign that a visiting priest had arrived unexpectedly and wanted to say mass; it was my duty to set out the vestments and the sacred vessels of the altar for the visitor. I was in a prolonged dried-out period at this time and was very short on patience. When I saw the sacristan heading my way, I could feel the indignation rising within me along with the commentary, "Here goes my prayer time again. Why can't the superiors give this job to somebody else?" Instead of being grateful for the honor of setting out the vestments, I was inwardly grumbling and murmuring against God. Thoughts of blasphemy sometimes swept over me. By this time I had enough faith to know that God was arranging everything in my life, so I would say, "Lord, why do you do this to me? Here I am trying to pray during the little free time that I have and you foul up the few chances I get." Then guilt feelings would immediately arise: "How can I have such thoughts when God is so good to me? I guess I don't have a vocation." Here an insidious voice would chime in, "You sure don't! This is no place for you!" The tempter was only too happy to reinforce my negative thoughts.

The third trial in the night of sense is similar to, and in fact antici-
pates, the later purification that John of the Cross calls the night of
spirit, in which one's inmost being is purged of the last traces of the
false self.

> At other times another abominable spirit, which Isaiah calls
> *Spiritus vertiginis,* [the Spirit of Dizziness] is allowed to molest
> them, not in order that they may fall, but that it may try them.
> This spirit darkens their senses in such a way that it fills them
> with numerous scruples and perplexities, so confusing that, as
> they judge, they can never, by any means, be satisfied concerning
> them, neither can they find any help for their judgment in counsel
> or thought. (*Dark Night of the Soul,* Ch. 14, no. 3)

This uncertainty could be about one's vocation or about some serious
matter of conscience. The afflicted person feels like a Ping-Pong ball
batted back and forth across the net. "Yes, I'll do this. No, I better do
something else. No, not that, but maybe this." Even when one goes to
a spiritual advisor and is told, "Here's the solution to your problem,"
peace lasts about a minute, and then one is back in the whirlpool of
uncertainty and may feel rejected or abandoned by God.

Why does God allow such excruciating trials? Notice that these
extreme temptations, like a spotlight on a dark stage, focus on the
selfishness that lies at the heart of each emotional program for
happiness.

The spirit of fornication reveals the intensity of desire that fuels our
instinctual need for pleasure, affection, and esteem. In the night of
sense, all sensible satisfactions dry out. If this situation is prolonged,
human nature craves to feel something—anything! It reaches out for
any pleasurable thing it can find. Sexual activity is for most people
the most pleasurable of sense experiences: hence, temptations of lust

may arise with great force. In others this craving for pleasure can also express itself in overeating, listening to certain kinds of music, or endlessly entertaining or distracting themselves—anything to get away from the interminable dryness.

The spirit of blasphemy addresses the need to control. In the night of sense, we cannot control anything. All our plans, including plans for self-improvement, come to nothing. This eventually causes intense frustration that may express itself in angry thoughts bordering on blasphemy. One would like to grab God by the throat and choke him.

The spirit of dizziness spotlights the need for certitude that is rooted in our security program. In this trial, we do not feel certitude about anything. The spiritual journey is a call into the unknown. Its scriptural paradigm is the call of Abraham: "Leave your father's house, your friends, relatives, and property, and come into the land that I will show you" (Gen. 12:1). God first calls us out of our childish ways of reacting into relationships that are appropriate for full mental egoic consciousness. But after that has been stabilized, we have not the remotest idea where God is taking us. Paul says, "Eye has not seen, ear has not heard, nor has it so much as dawned on man what God has prepared for those who love him" (1 Cor. 2:9). The only way to get there is to consent not to know. The desire or demand for certitude is an obstacle to launching full sail on the ocean of trust.

These three trials are immense favors from God. The divine light puts the spotlight on the source of the problem, which is the innate selfishness that is the hard core of each of the emotional programs for happiness. We cannot bring the false self to an end by ourselves; we can only allow it to die. If we do what we can to dismantle it, God, in response to our efforts, moves in and completes the job. All we have to do then is to consent. But that is about the biggest job there is. When all our efforts have failed, we finally accept the gift of God's infinite mercy.

The night of sense enables us to perceive that the source of the emotional programs for happiness is selfishness. By letting go of our desires for satisfaction in these areas, we move toward a permanent disposition of peace. Upsetting thoughts and emotions arise, but they no longer build up into emotional binges. The immense energy that was required to bear the afflictive emotions that flared up when our programs for happiness were frustrated is now available for more useful things, such as loving the people with whom we live and whom we are trying to serve.

13

Anthony in the Tombs

Freedom from Cultural Conditioning

Periods of struggle move us to new levels of integration, and then we have to translate our relationships to God, ourselves, and other people into this new perspective. This may take some years. After it has been accomplished, the spiritual food that nourishes us at that level eventually becomes insipid and no longer nourishes. We find ourselves once again in a crisis of faith, and, after another extended struggle, we take the leap to the next level of faith and love. This does not mean that we are immediately well established at the new level. Rather, we must go through another lengthy period of integrating all our relationships into the new perspective.

So it was for Anthony. After the first round of battles with the demons, Anthony emerged into a period of relative tranquility and inner equilibrium—a plateau, as John of the Cross would call it. The plateau refers to the sense of freedom that emerges after the purification of the false self. But such a purification is not the end of the journey. Anthony knew that the devil was plotting further strategies against him. Accordingly, he did not presume on any progress he had made, but began anew each day, as if he were at the very beginning of the journey.

As Anthony completed the period of integration, he began to feel within himself a further call into the unknown, an invitation to take another quantum leap of trust in God. In Anthony's story we read this simple phrase: "Anthony left for the tombs which lay at some distance from the village" (*The Life of St. Anthony*, No. 8, 26).[1] If we were fourth-century readers, our hair would be standing on end at these words. "He's going to the tombs!" we would exclaim in disbelief. In the popular imagination, the tombs, and especially the desert, were believed to be the strongholds of the demons. No one ever stayed in the tombs longer than was necessary to lay a deceased relative or friend on a shelf.

This one sentence in Anthony's story may represent a whole year or longer during which Anthony was trying to discern whether he should take his battles with the devil into the latter's territory. In the end, Anthony decided to take the offensive. Going to the tombs was thus an expression of tremendous courage, a stepping forth from the cultural conditioning of his time and place in complete disregard of the popular mindset.

As we have seen, Anthony was probably withdrawn and timid by temperament. He may have realized that there was still some residue of timidity in his character, and felt inspired by God to confront it. The difference between Anthony and certain starry-eyed ascetics is that his decision was an inspiration of grace. Some people attempt to imitate those who are advanced in the spiritual journey before they have taken their own first steps. They want to become perfect all at once and take on penances, trials, and ministries that are beyond their capacities. They usually fall on their noses. We cannot expect God to support us if we are doing our own thing. The spiritual journey consists in doing God's thing.

The decision to take the battle into the devil's territory is a vivid symbol of the struggle to free oneself from cultural overidentification.

Mythic membership consciousness, we have seen, is characterized by overidentification with the value systems of a particular group. In this case, the culture, by giving power to the devil over certain places or geographical locations, was limiting the sphere of God's love and power. To become free—that is, to move from mythic membership to mental egoic consciousness—requires a journey away from cultural expectations, stereotypes, and mindsets into an increasing trust in the goodness and power of God.

Anthony marched off alone to the tombs and asked a friend to lock him in. Notice that detail. Was he afraid that his resolution would weaken?

Anthony's courage took the devil by surprise. I paraphrase his words: "What is this guy doing here? How dare he set foot in my domain? Let's get rid of him!" With this the devil called all his cohorts together and they beat Anthony into semiconsciousness. Anthony said afterward that no human force could have beaten him so badly. His friend, when he came to bring Anthony some bread, found him lying on the ground unconscious. The friend picked Anthony up, carried him to the church, and laid him on the ground. His relatives and friends gathered around his body and mourned him as if he were a corpse.

Toward midnight, however, they all started to doze. Anthony awoke and saw that they were nodding. The question must have risen in his mind, "What is the Spirit asking of me now? Is he saying, 'You have done enough, call an ambulance and go to the hospital'? Or is he saying, 'Anthony, it is time to bring this battle to a conclusion; go back, I'll take care of you'?"

This was Anthony's double bind. "Shall I return? Shall I not? Is this an inspiration coming from God, or is it just my idea?" He decided in favor of taking the risk. He beckoned to his friend and asked to be carried back to the tombs. His friend lifted him quietly so that no one would wake up, carried him to the tombs, laid him on the floor, and once again locked the door and departed. (One wonders what kind of friend this was.)

Anthony was too feeble to stand, so he prayed lying down. Having finished his prayer, he challenged the devil as follows: "Here I am!" he shouted. "I am not cowed by your blows. Even though you should give me more, nothing can separate me from the love of Christ." Then, as was his custom, he began to sing verses of the psalms. "If camps of enemies stand against me, my heart shall not fear" (Ps. 27:3). Notice the reference to fear, suggesting his determination to eliminate the last traces of fear so that he might be completely free to follow every movement of the Spirit.

Athanasius writes: "The hater of good marveled that after all the blows Anthony had the courage to come back." The devil called together his "dogs" (a nickname for the demons among the Desert Fathers) and, bursting with rage, shouted, "You see that we have not stopped this fellow, neither by the spirit of fornication, nor by blows. On the contrary, he even challenges us! Let us go after him in another way!"

That night they made such a din that the place seemed to be shaken by an earthquake. It was as though the demons were bursting through the four walls of the little chamber in the form of beasts and reptiles. All at once the place was filled with the phantoms of lions, bears, leopards, bulls, serpents, asps, scorpions, and wolves. Each moved according to the shape it had assumed. The lion roared ready to spring. The bull appeared about to gore him through. The serpent writhed ready to strike him. The noises emitted simultaneously by all the apparitions were frightful, and the fury shown was fierce. Anthony, pummeled and goaded, felt even more severe pain in his body, yet he lay there fearless. (*The Life of St. Anthony,* No. 9, 27ff.)

Notice the last word "fearless," hinting that Anthony has now passed beyond the dimension of fear. The text continues:

But he was all the more alert in spirit. He groaned because of the pain that racked his body, but his mind was master of the situation. And to mock them, he said, "If you had any power, it would have been enough for just one of you to come. You are just trying to scare me out of my wits. If you have received power against me, come at me. If you cannot, why excite yourselves to no purpose?" After many ruses, the demons gnashed their teeth against him because they were only fooling themselves and not him. The Lord was not forgetful of Anthony's struggle, but came to help him. For Anthony looked up and saw, as it were, the roof opening and a beam of light coming down to him. The demons suddenly were gone. The pain in his body ceased. The building was restored to its former condition. Anthony, perceiving that help had come, breathed more freely and felt relieved of his pains. (*The Life of St. Anthony,* No. 9, 27ff)

He asked the vision the inevitable question that arises in such circumstances:

Where were *you?* Why did you not appear at the beginning to stop my pains? And a voice came to him, "Anthony, I was right here, but I waited to see you in action. And now because you held out and did not surrender, I will always be your helper and I will make you renowned everywhere. (*The Life of St. Anthony,* No. 10, 28)

The last line is reminiscent of the promises God made to Abraham after he came through his great trial of faith on Mount Horeb.

> Hearing this, Anthony rose in prayer. He was so strengthened that he felt his body more vigorous than before. He was at this time about thirty-five years of age. (*The Life of St. Anthony*, No. 10, 28)

The question and the Lord's answer linger in my mind with a certain uneasiness. Is the answer "I was right here watching to see you in action" convincing? Why could God not have come a little sooner, as Anthony suggested? Anyone in straits such as Anthony was in would feel completely abandoned by God. Where was God's infinite compassion? He did not seem to provide any help at all.

In the presence of immense suffering, any attempt to answer on God's behalf sounds like a platitude. In place of an answer, I offer this parable based on a story by Gerald Heard called "Dryness and the Dark Night":[2]

A certain scientist devoted his life to developing a strain of butterfly that would be the most beautiful combination of colors ever seen on this planet. After years of experimentation, he was certain that he had a cocoon that would produce his genetic masterpiece. On the day that the butterfly was expected to emerge, he gathered together his entire staff. All waited breathlessly as the creature began to work its way out of the cocoon. It disengaged its right wing, its body, and most of its left wing. Just as the staff were ready to cheer and pass the champagne and cigars, they saw with horror that the extremity of the left wing of the butterfly was stuck in the mouth of the cocoon. The creature was desperately flapping its other wing to free itself. As it labored, it grew more and more exhausted. Each new effort seemed more difficult, and the intervals between efforts grew longer. At last the scientist, unable to bear the tension, took a scalpel and cut a tiny section from the mouth of the cocoon. With one final burst of strength, the butterfly fell free onto the laboratory table. Everybody cheered and reached for the cigars and the champagne. Then silence again descended on the room. Although the butterfly was free, it could not fly. . .

The struggle to escape from the cocoon is nature's way of forcing blood to the extremities of a butterfly's wings so that when it emerges from the cocoon it can enjoy its new life and fly to its heart's content. In seeking to save the creature's life, the scientist had truncated its capacity to function. A butterfly that cannot fly is a contradiction in terms.

This is a mistake that God is not going to make. The image of God watching Anthony has to be understood. God holds back his infinite mercy from rushing to the rescue when we are in temptation and difficulties. He will not actively intervene because the struggle is opening and preparing every recess of our being for the divine energy of grace. God is transforming us so that we can enjoy the divine life to the full once it has been established. If the divine help comes too soon, before the work of purification and healing has been accomplished, it may frustrate our ultimate ability to live the divine life.

Anthony's battles with the devil were not yet over. Athanasius's text continues, "On the next day, Anthony went out inspired with an even greater zeal for the service of God." He headed for the desert. In the fourth century, the desert was believed to be the stronghold of the devil, his military-industrial complex, so to speak, where he devised projects to destroy lives, communities, and nations, worldwide.

Thus, Anthony marched into the devil's concentration of power. It is a mistake to think of monastic life as an escape from the world. Monasticism is the aggressive action of persons who struggle with the "evil powers in high places" that Paul writes about, in order to wrench from them their insidious ascendancy over the human family. The ascesis of solitude is not kindergarten; it is postgraduate work in the spiritual journey. Significantly, Anthony lodged in an abandoned fort, symbol of the devil's ammunition dump. As he went in, the reptiles that were living there went out as fast as they could. Anthony again asked his friend to lock him in, and there he stayed, seeing no one and continuously doing battle with the demons.

He spent the next twenty years in the fort. His friends sometimes came and, listening at the door, thought there was a riot going on inside. The demons, however, were not getting the better of Anthony; they were trying to escape from him! Anthony prayed various verses from the psalms to force them to relinquish their grip over the people they were oppressing. He loved such verses as, "Let God arise and his enemies be scattered. As the smoke vanishes, so let them vanish away," and, "All nations compassed me about. In the name of the Lord, I drove them off."

When Anthony was fifty-five years of age, his friends tore down the door of the fort. Anthony took this as the call of God to emerge from his solitude.

Anthony came forth as out of a shrine, as one initiated into the sacred mysteries and filled with the Spirit of God. When his friends saw him, they were astonished that his body had kept its former appearance. He was neither fat from want of exercise, nor emaciated from fasting and struggles. He was the same man they had known before his retirement. Again the state of his soul was pure for it was neither contracted by grief, nor dissipated by pleasure, nor pervaded by jollity. He was not embarrassed when he saw the crowd, nor was he elated at seeing so many there to receive him. He had himself completely under control, a man guided by reason and stable in his character. He exhorted all to prefer nothing in the world to the love of Christ. (*The Life of St. Anthony,* No. 14, 32)

The desert that had once belonged to the demons now became a place of peace. In a decade it was filled with thousands of monks.

Anthony's experience of the spiritual journey is a classic example of how the divine action works in our lives. When he reacted vigorously against the devil's first temptation to abandon the spiritual journey and return to a worldly life, he entered the night of sense, during which time the divine action laid to rest the unconscious motivation of his false self. Having enjoyed a plateau in which he worked his newfound freedom into ordinary daily life and his relationships, he moved into a further confrontation with the devil, which was at the same time a radical letting go of the influence of his cultural conditioning insofar as it was an obstacle to following Christ. John of the Cross calls this purification the night of spirit, a transitional period that will be considered more fully in chapter fifteen. From this decisive trial, he entered the transforming union.

14

The Fruits of the
Night of Sense

The night of sense is about dismantling our immature programs for happiness, which can't possibly work in adult life. Little do we realize when we embark on the spiritual journey that our first fervor is itself immature and under the influence of these programs; it will have some growing up to do.

Thus, at some point in our journey, a pervasive sense of God's absence begins to manifest itself during prayer and spreads into other areas of one's life. This is actually the beginning of a deeper union with Christ. Most of us, however, do not experience it that way. When the biblical desert opens up within us, we worry that something is going wrong in our relationship with God.

In the night of sense, we are called to make the transition from superficial spiritual nourishment to the solid food of pure faith. The sensible consolations enjoyed during prayer, liturgy, or *lectio divina* may be compared to junk food. We are now being served much more substantial food, the dry bread of faith. The baby weaned from its mother's breast does not like the privation of its customary nourishment, but solid food will lead to more substantial growth. Similarly, God as divine mother pushes us away from the breasts of consolation so that we can adjust to the pure food of faith that will strengthen us for the rugged terrain of the spiritual journey.

The night of sense heals the malformations that took place in growing from childhood to early adolescence when we felt that our basic needs were not being met and we responded with insatiable compensatory demands. We not only experience dryness in our relationship with God, but also a lack of satisfaction in all the areas in which we previously sought happiness. When the emotional programs dry out and begin to crumble, they make a last stand to resist their demise.

The principle fruit of the night of sense is humility, which enables us to assume our places as members of the human family, enduring the ups and downs of the human condition like everybody else. Actually, God is giving us more protection than before, though in secret.

The night of sense is designed to bring about the dismantling of the emotional programs and the death of the false self. The fruit of this purifying process is the freedom to decide what to do, without interference from the compulsions and fixations of the false self. It took constant effort to keep ourselves in some semblance of peace when we were seeking fantastic goals that were constantly frustrated, setting off the afflictive emotions of anger, grief, fear, pride, lust, greed, jealousy, and the other capital sins. As the false self diminishes and trust in God increases in the night of sense, our energies can be put to better purposes.

The night of sense is doing more than dismantling the false self. In relaxing our compulsions and habitual ways of overreacting, it also releases the energies of the unconscious. This is particularly true if our journey is grounded in the regular practice of contemplative prayer by a receptive method such as Centering Prayer. Through the process of resting in God, beyond thoughts, feeling, associations, and commentaries, we are moving from the level of our physical faculties and their perceptions to the level of the spiritual faculties and their intuitions, and opening to the divine presence at a deeper level still. This brings even greater rest. And this rest, in turn, loosens up the material in the unconscious that the defense mechanisms of early childhood have previously kept out of our awareness.

The energies of the unconscious may rise to awareness in either a positive or a negative way. Psychic powers and spiritual consolations generally produce positive emotions. Negative emotions arise when the dark sides of our personalities and our mixed motivations thrust themselves into our awareness, alerting us to the damage that the false self is doing.

A number of seekers have experienced a sudden upsurge of powerful energy without being adequately prepared for it. In some cases it was triggered by a mantra or set of breathing exercises specifically designed to loosen up the energies of the unconscious. If we experience spiritual consolation, psychic powers, or charismatic gifts before the purification of pride in the night of sense, we could be overwhelmed by feelings of self-exaltation; if the dark sides of our personalities arise, we could be submerged in the depths of discouragement.

The antidote for this naïveté is sound spiritual teaching. All the great spiritual traditions of the world religions require both devotion to God and the service of others as two essential practices for beginners. For the Christian, devotion and dedication to God are cultivated in the practice of *lectio divina* (a sacred, attentive listening to the word of God through scripture), liturgy, and prayer. We grow in the service of others through the fulfillment of the duties of our state of life, whatever these may be. The building up of these two banks, as it were, creates a safe channel for the emergence of the positive and negative contents of the unconscious. It prepares us to benefit from the various forms of self-knowledge revealed by the night of sense and avoids the hazards of repressed material exploding into consciousness before we have established an adequate discipline and the proper attitudes to handle it.

A positive benefit derived from the energies arising from the unconscious is the development of the intuitive level of consciousness. According to Ken Wilber's model (see Appendix III), this level transcends even the mental egoic and opens up a new perspective on all reality. The human brain has potentialities that are still waiting to be actualized. If we can believe the experience of many mystics, the present level of human consciousness is the door to higher states of consciousness. In their view, our human potentialities are only fully realized in the transforming union.

In mythic membership consciousness, we absorb unquestioningly the values of parents, nation, race, and early religious education. These unquestioned assumptions become our world view, or the myth in which we live. In the night of sense, these presuppositions are challenged, though not as deeply as they will be in the night of spirit. Like the parables of Jesus, the night of sense shakes the ground on which we had felt secure and opens us to new ways of seeing reality.

At each level of human development, God offers himself to us just as we are. Thus, he is the typhonic God of primitive peoples and children, the monotheistic God of mythic membership consciousness, and the God of infinite concern for the whole human family revealed in the gospel. Each of us, in growing up, relates to God on each of these levels.

In the night of sense, our primitive ideas of God are challenged. The latter may include prejudices imposed on us in early childhood. If God was presented as a tyrant, policeman, or implacable judge, the emotional overtones of these frightening images may remain deeply ingrained. They are emotional judgments, not true judgments, and need to be corrected. The night of sense enables us to face our distorted views of God and to lay them aside. Then we are free to relate to God as he is and to use the immense energy that this freedom releases to relate to other people with respect and love.

One way God deals with the limited ways we have of relating to him is by reducing our concepts of him to silence. As resting in God in contemplative prayer becomes habitual, we spontaneously disidentify with our emotional programs for happiness and our cultural conditioning. Already we are meeting God at a deeper level. In time we will grow from a reflective relationship with God to one of communion. The latter is a being-to-being, presence-to-presence relationship, which is the knowledge of God in pure faith.

The night of sense brings the nature of commitment into clear focus. When we take to heart Jesus' words, "Follow me," he invites us into his friendship. Friendship always involves commitment to the other person. This is the disposition that enabled Anthony to get through all his temptations and to reach transforming union. His basic means were always the same: commitment to the spiritual journey, the practice of constant prayer, and trust that God would give him the strength to persevere.

The apparent absences of God, interior purification, and the trials of daily life challenge our commitment. In our time, models of commitment are few. People move from job to job; marriages do not last; careers end prematurely; religious life and vows of celibacy are not taken as seriously as they used to be. The supports that once helped or forced people to remain in their commitments have diminished through the cultural revolutions of modern times. Whatever good has come from these social developments, the models of commitment available in earlier times have largely disappeared, at least in the Western world.

Most young married couples do not have the remotest idea of what they are getting into at the times of their weddings. When difficulties arise, they often decide that they were not cut out for each other and call it quits. They go through heartrending divorces and seek other mates, only to repeat the same horrendous process. Of course, there are some committed relationships that do die or become harmful. Other relationships are dominated by the romantic side alone and disintegrate in the face of the demands of love that require self-sacrifice.

Actually, difficulties arise whenever a committed relationship is succeeding. Love makes you vulnerable. When you feel loved by God or by another person, you do not have to be self-protective. Your defenses relax and the dark side of your personality arises, not only into consciousness, but also into your behavior, to the dismay, perhaps, of your spouse. Hopefully, your spouse is having similar experiences. One purpose of the sacrament of marriage is to provide the grace to process each other's dark side. In this way, marriage becomes a school of purification and transformation. When a couple bears with each other's failures, dark sides, and weaknesses, they minister the love of God to each other. Human love is the symbol of God's love in the sacrament of marriage and communicates it to the other person. The commitment to marriage enables one to get through the process of self-knowledge and to reap the benefit of this enlightenment.

Suppose that you become aware that your motives for entering marriage were defective. If you are a man, maybe you were looking for the mamma that you never had or for a replica of the mamma you *did* have and saw in this capable person someone who would take care of all your needs: do the wash, put food on the table every day, and dry your tears. Suddenly, it dawns on you, precisely because of your progress in self-knowledge, that this was not the right motive to marry in the first place. So the thought comes, "The only way to gain my freedom is to sever this relationship completely." But the commitment suggests, "Why not bring your new insight back into the relationship and see if it can now work?" This is not always possible because the patterns of dependency may be too deeply ingrained. Separating may indeed be necessary when a serious mistake is made, but the commitment inclines us first to try to bring the new insight into the relationship.

No one enters a commitment, including the religious life or priesthood, with completely pure motives. Thus, it is not so much the motives we had in entering, but the motives we have for persevering that actually count the most.

God is calling us in the night of sense to take responsibility for ourselves and for our personal response to Christ's invitation to follow him. This includes our response to the people we live with and, ultimately, to the whole human family.

As the night of sense gradually turns to dust all our previous sources of strength and consolation, the temptation to give up is enormous. "This journey can't be for me. I have a family to raise, a professional life to lead. I can't deal with all this painful negativity that keeps rising within me." When dryness and temptation are prolonged, everything in us wants to call a halt to the spiritual journey and hopes we never have to start again. If we walk away from our commitment to the journey, the false self goes with us. Wherever we go, we will have to face it again under other circumstances. Commitment opposes this regressive instinct, saying, "I won't give up. I resolve for the love of Christ to go through the desert of purification no matter what happens." This is the determination that enables the night of sense to complete its work.

15

The Stages of Contemplative Prayer

In the night of sense, God is feeding us from within rather than engaging our faculties through the external senses, memory, imagination, and reason. In contemplative prayer these faculties are at rest so that our intuitive faculties, the passive intellect, and the will-to-God, may access the "still point," the place where our personal identity is rooted in God as an abiding presence. The divine presence has always been with us, but we think it is absent. That thought is the monumental illusion of the human condition. The spiritual journey is designed to heal it.

We translate dryness in prayer as God's absence until we perceive that God is communicating with us at a deeper level. Silence is God's first language; everything else is a poor translation. In order to hear that language, we must learn to be still and to rest in God. One of the signs of the night of sense is an inclination for solitude and silence; to be alone with God, even though we do not find any satisfaction in it. The vague but felt need for God comes from the contemplative gifts of the Spirit, especially the gift of knowledge, which relativizes all other goods and announces the onset of the night of sense.

The attraction to interior silence is the result of the food of pure faith that God is communicating, not to the senses or to reason, but to our intuitive faculties. At first we do not know what to do with this dryness; hence, the disconcerting reactions that make us want to give up the whole process of prayer in favor of relaxation or some form of engrossing work. As we accustom ourselves to the exercise of pure faith, however, we begin to experience its fruits: trust in God and humility. The latter manifests itself in an unwillingness to judge others. Our own good deeds appear so mixed with selfish motivations that we would be happy if no one would ever bring them up again. We are painfully aware of the fact that all our actions are shot through with selfishness and that, try as we may, we cannot do much about it.

At this point, the spiritual journey may begin to unfold along the lines that the sixteenth-century Spanish mystic Saint Teresa of Avila described in *The Interior Castle*. She presented the spiritual journey from the perspective of the stages of prayer. This is indeed the way that many people experience the journey. There is an alternative, but let us look first at Teresa's model.

The first grace that emerges as the night of sense nears its completion is a mysterious awakening, as if a breath of fresh air has entered one's spirit. A whiff of the divine perfume escapes from God's presence at the inmost center of our being and comes within range of our spiritual faculties. Teresa of Avila calls this grace "infused recollection." This term is confusing because every kind of prayer has an infused element—i.e., it is given to us; we do not manufacture it. God was present in the night of sense, but we had not recognized his presence and thought he was absent. Now the former dryness seems to have a delicious spiritual savor that attracts us toward the center of our being. Spiritual consolation does not come through the external senses; it wells up from a source deep within. It may overflow into the senses like a fountain, but the source of the water does not spring from sense or rational activity.

Infused recollection does not absorb us in such a way that we cannot resist; we can get up and walk away. Normally, the feeling is so pleasant that we want to prolong it. This grace may expand into the prayer of quiet in which the will is absorbed in God. The faculties of memory and imagination are free to roam around and often play with images and memories in order to keep themselves occupied. The will feels persecuted by their unwanted activity. Teresa says that we should regard the wanderings of memory and imagination as "the ravings of a madman," and pay no attention to them. Thus, we may experience a bombardment of thoughts that we do not want, while at the same time our will is attending to the presence of God, whether through an undifferentiated sense of unity or a more personal attention to one or another of the Divine Persons.

The "prayer of quiet," the next stage, is more absorbing than infused recollection. In this state the divine action seems to grasp the will in a spiritual embrace. The will could break away but does not want to. In fact, it easily becomes attached to the feeling of consolation and wants to prolong the time of prayer. When prayer is delightful, we want more of it. Thus we may fall into the trap of spiritual gluttony and try to squeeze as much pleasure as we can out of this God who has suddenly become so bountiful.

If the prayer of quiet moves to a yet deeper level, the imagination and memory are temporarily suspended. God, as it were, calls these faculties to himself. They hear the sound of his voice and are enchanted by it; they gather around and sit still to listen. While they are quiet, the will enjoys the divine presence. In that state God can communicate more of his gifts because there is no resistance or commentary on our side. This is the "prayer of union."

In all these states, we are aware of the presence of something real, but it is not a form, image, or concept. The divine presence may arise in various ways. It can come suddenly or overtake us gradually. It may seem to descend from above or arise from below. It may envelop us like a luminous cloud or well up from within. In any case, there is a sense of deep quiet as the imagination and memory grow still. When they are completely still and the will is totally absorbed in God, there is no self-reflection. This is the experience of the "prayer of full union" in which all the faculties are motionless and rest in God.

John of the Cross also describes this process, but indicates that there is another path, which he calls the path of pure faith. Both paths move toward the goal of transforming union, which is the abiding sense of rootedness in the divine presence within. John refers to the path of pure faith as a "hidden ladder." This is the path that people on the spiritual journey experience most of the time. They have the attraction for interior prayer, but do not experience the levels of absorption described by Teresa. At times they are aware that their will is resting in God, but their habitual experience is dryness accompanied by endless wanderings of the imagination. Even when the night of sense is far advanced, their prayer may continue without any noticeable change.

Certain spiritual writers have identified what might be called the "felt" experience of God with contemplative prayer to such an extent that when it is absent they presume that contemplation is also absent. John of the Cross, as well as experience, disproves this theory. There is an exuberant approach to divine union that is full of light, and there is an approach that is very dark. In other words, we may be invited to the front entrance of the interior castle, or we may be directed to the service entrance. We may be invited to climb the front stairs, or we may be led up the back stairs. The back stairs correspond to the hidden ladder of John of the Cross. Which way is better? Nobody knows. What is certain is that both paths lead to transforming union. God as he is in himself can be fully accessed only by pure faith. The purification of faith and love, not spiritual consolation, leads to transforming union.

Transforming union is a restructuring of consciousness, not an experience or set of experiences. In the course of this restructuring, as we shall see in chapter sixteen, the presence of God becomes a kind of fourth dimension to the three-dimensional world in which we have been living. In the light of transforming union, therefore, the most important element in centering prayer is the practice itself, not its psychological content. If we fully grasped this truth, it would make the spiritual journey much easier. At the beginning of the journey, our expectations of what should happen and our commentaries about what is happening are the causes of most of our anxiety and distress.

For those enjoying the path of exuberant mysticism, as well for those on the hidden ladder, there comes the further purification of the night of spirit. Even in the experience of the unfolding stages of prayer, the false self is at work, subtly transferring its worldly desires for satisfaction to the good things that are now available on the spiritual path. This last assertion is not meant to denigrate the value of the consolations of contemplative prayer. Some people need them, especially those who have been severely damaged in childhood. God bends over, caresses, and virtually makes love to people who have been deeply hurt, in order to convince them that it is all right to enjoy pleasures that they thought they should not enjoy, or were taught that they should not enjoy. God invites them to review the emotional judgments of childhood and to accept the good things of life with grateful hearts. Gratitude is an essential disposition in the spiritual journey.

The experience of God's love enables us to understand emotionally where true values are to be found. When we taste the goodness of God and experience the humility that arises spontaneously from that relationship, the programs glorified by the false self and our cultural conditioning diminish in size and no longer exercise the fascination that used to hold them in place.

16

The Night of Spirit

As have seen, the night of sense virtually immobilizes the false self. Its residue, however, is still lingering in our spiritual faculties and manifests itself by the secret satisfaction that we find in ourselves as the recipients of God's favors or of a special vocation. It is all very well to say, "I owe everything to God." But there may still be a subtle inclination that says, "After all, he did give these gifts to *me*!" The tendency to possess even on the spiritual level requires purification. This is the work of the night of spirit.

The night of spirit, the beginning of divine union according to John of the Cross, is a further transitional stage involving a more intimate purification. John teaches that even during the experience of exuberant mysticism there are "alarms." We become aware that there are some rough spots in the unconscious that have not been corrected by the night of sense, such as habitual distractedness of mind, the lingering effects of cultural conditioning, and spiritual pride. The night of spirit is designed to free us from the residue of the false self in the unconscious and thus to prepare us for divine union.

When the night of spirit begins, all "felt" mystical experiences of God subside and disappear, leaving persons who have been led by the path of exuberant mysticism in a state of intense longing to have them back. In proportion to the spiritual consolations that these persons previously received, they now experience the pain of privation. Perhaps the night of spirit is less painful for those who are led by the hidden ladder since they do not enjoy much, if any, of God's felt presence. In any case, the night of spirit is essential for the final movement into divine union. Without that purification, the consequences of the false self are not completely erased, and there is danger of falling into the negative energies that may arise out of the unconscious.

Those who have been led by the path of exuberant mysticism are especially susceptible to these subtle temptations. They may experience psychic or spiritual gifts and become gifted teachers or charismatic leaders. But the very gifts that attract people to them and to their teaching subtly and insidiously incline them toward a glamorous self-image. Precisely because of their spiritual attainments, the temptation arises to identify with the role of prophet, wonderworker, enlightened teacher, martyr, victim, charismatic leader—in short, God's gift to humanity. The night of spirit reduces such temptations to zero because, through its purifying action, we experience ourselves as capable of every evil. Not that we are likely to commit evil deeds, but we feel completely dependent on God in order to avoid personal sin or the habitual hang-ups of the false self that lead to it.

This kind of temptation is important to understand in our time when a lot of publicity is given to psychic gifts such as out-of-body experiences, channeling, levitation, control of bodily functions, various forms of healing, prophecy, and many others. Spiritually gifted people may also be empowered to impart spiritual experiences to others. The latter takes place in the charismatic renewal in the phenomenon called "slaying in the Spirit." Unfortunately, if enlightenment is only partial, success and adulation may go to some people's heads; then the temptation to identify with a particular idealized self-image takes over, and they are back in the grip of the false self.

Service is the hallmark of one who is sent by God. The true prophet, martyr, spiritual leader, or teacher does not try to dominate others. Notice how often Jesus emphasized that he was sent by his Father and that he did nothing of himself: "He can do only what he sees the Father doing" (John 5:19). His chief argument against every accusation was, "My Father is at work until now, and I am at work as well" (John 8:16).

In a ministry inspired by God, one receives a particular call and has to exercise it on God's terms. That means that the ministry will be characterized, as it was for Jesus, by opposition, rejection, failure, disappointment, persecution, and perhaps death. Jesus did not invoke his psychic powers or his prerogatives as the Son of God to defend himself or his teaching. He allowed himself to experience the utmost suffering and rejection as part of being sent, thus manifesting the inner nature of Ultimate Reality as infinite compassion and forgiveness. His death and resurrection put an enormous question mark in front of everything the false self looks upon as happiness or success.

The spiritual journey is not a success story, but a series of diminutions of self. Saint Bernard of Clairvaux, the twelfth-century Cistercian abbot, taught that humiliation is the path to humility. In those who have a low self-image, there may be some confusion between humility and the neurotic tendency to put oneself down. The latter, of course, is not humility. The language of humility can be misunderstood. Basically, it is the experiential awareness, born of the divine light, that without God's protection we are capable of every sin. The night of the spirit is an intensive course in humility.

There are five significant fruits of the night of spirit. The first fruit is freedom from the temptation to assume a glamorous role because of our spiritual gifts or charisms. It purifies the secret satisfaction of being chosen as the recipient of God's special gifts. It allows God to treat us like everyone else and allows us to find his special love in that treatment, rather than in experiences that single us out from the rest of humanity. Christ represented us on the cross and identified with the consequences of sin, the chief of which is the sense of abandonment by God. It is in the sacrifice of his divine prerogatives that he became the savior of the world and entered into the fullness of his glory, not by earthly success or by taking to himself a role that was not given to him.

The second fruit of the night of spirit is freedom from the domination of any emotion. Characteristically, we are pushed around by emotions and by our tendency to overidentify with them, and we find ourselves forever trying to get what they want or to get away from what they do not want. The night of spirit gradually frees us from the last traces of domination by emotional swings or moods. This takes place not by repressing or unduly suppressing unwanted emotions by sheer willpower, but by accepting and integrating them into the rational and intuitive parts of our nature. The emotions will then serve and support the decisions of reason and will, which is their natural purpose. The integration of our emotional life with reason and faith and the subjection of our whole being to God constitute Saint Thomas Aquinas's definition of human happiness. In his view, human beings were meant to act in harmony with their nature and to enjoy doing so. This harmonious state is substantially restored in the night of spirit by extinguishing the last traces of our subjection to the emotional programs for happiness in the spiritual part of our nature. As for the emotional and sense levels, they were laid to rest in the night of sense.

The third fruit of the night of spirit is the purification of our idea of God, the God of our childhood or the God worshipped by the particular group to which we belong. The God we used to know no longer seems to care about us. In addition, God even purifies the idea of him that we developed through the experience of close union enjoyed during the period of exuberant mysticism (if that was our path). God reveals himself in the night of spirit in a vastly superior way—as infinite, incomprehensible, and ineffable—the way that he appeared to Moses on Mount Sinai and to Elijah on Mount Horeb. No one can describe the experience of pure faith. We know only that an immense and unnameable energy is welling up inside. This immense energy may be experienced by some as impersonal, although it certainly treats us in a personal way.

The fourth fruit of the night of spirit is the purification of what are traditionally known as the "theological virtues," which are faith, hope, and love. In the purification of faith from human props, we may experience rejection by the group from whom we have been drawing our human, religious, or spiritual identity. There may be a breakup with our spiritual director or with people on whom we depended for spiritual development and for meaning in life. Our idea of the spiritual journey and the means we should use to pursue it, and our ideas of our vocations, the Church, Jesus Christ—even God himself—may be shattered. This experience is reflected in the great personages of scripture like Job, Moses, Joseph, Mary, and Jesus himself. Jesus' life and teaching were built on his personal union with the Father, and yet, in his last moments, he seems to have experienced that relationship as a gigantic question mark. "My God, my God, why have you forsaken me?" Job, according to the biblical story, was a model of perfection and admired by everyone in his time. In the course of a few days, his property, family, reputation, and even his bodily health were swept away. What kind of God is this who permits or sends such tragedy into the lives of his friends? Job complained bitterly about his pitiful condition. But would he have learned who God is unless he had gone through the shattering experiences that brought to an end his naive conception of how God functions? The greatest fruit of the night of spirit is the disposition that is willing to accept God on his own terms. As a result, one allows God to be God without knowing who or what that is.

Total self-surrender and abandonment grow mightily, though in a manner hidden from us, in the night of spirit. The divine light is so pure that it is imperceptible to any of our faculties. According to John of the Cross, pure faith is a ray of darkness. Since there is no consolation or reassurance from God and since the props on which we used to rely have all been taken away, this surrender may be a moment of existential doubt and dread in the extreme. If we can let God be whoever God is and accept whatever he is doing, an invincible trust emerges. Such trust is not based on our good deeds, roles, or anything else. We simply trust in God's infinite mercy. Mercy of its nature reaches out to weakness and extreme need. We begin to be content with God's infinite mercy. Divine love is infused in the seedbed of total submission and self-surrender and brings us through the night of spirit into the transforming union.

The fifth fruit of the night of spirit is the longing to let go of the selfishness that still lingers in us and to be free of every obstacle that might hinder our growth in divine union. According to John of the Cross, the same fire of divine love that is experienced painfully in the night of spirit becomes gentle and full of love in the transforming union. The "I" of self-centeredness diminishes to a very small "i." The great "I AM" of Exodus looms in its place. Thus, the divine plan is to transform human nature into the divine, not by giving it some special role or exceptional powers, but by enabling it to live ordinary life with extraordinary love.

One final word of caution is in order. While we may talk of the divine "plan" and outline the stages of the spiritual journey as presented by the great teachers of our tradition, the only thing we can be absolutely sure of in the spiritual journey is that whatever we are expecting to happen will not happen. God is not bound by our ideas. Sometimes the night of sense begins at once, sometimes the night of sense and the night of spirit are reversed, and sometimes they take place at the same time. If we have read widely and expect that things are going to proceed according to our understanding, God will reverse the normal order for our benefit. One way or another, we will have to take the leap of trust into the unknown.

17

The Transforming Union

The experience of the transforming union is a way of being in the world that enables us to live daily life with the invincible conviction of continuous union with God. It is a new way of being in the world, a way of transcending everything in the world without leaving it.

In the transforming union, the domination of the emotions ceases. Emotional swings disappear. We are aware that what we thought were emotions were not the emotions as such, but our interpretations of them. The emotions are just as strong as ever and more so, but there is no backwash from them in the sense of lingering feelings or mood swings. The emotions are appropriate responses to the present moment with its specific content. Jesus in anger casting out the money changers is an example of this. When the situation is over, so is the emotional response. As a result, the emotions ho longer attract us to sinful activity. We are aware that we could still sin, but there is no stimulation to do so. Freedom from the false self and emotional domination is complete.

The Fathers of the Desert had a word for this experience. They called it "apatheia," which is sometimes taken to mean "indifference." It is rather a tremendous concern for everything that is, but without the emotional involvement characteristic of the false self. We are free to devote ourselves to the needs of others without becoming unduly absorbed in their emotional pain. We are present to people at the deepest level and perceive the presence of Christ suffering in them. We long to share with them something of the inner freedom we have been given, but without anxiety and without trying to change them or to obtain anything from them. We simply have the divine life as sheer gift and offer it to anyone who wants it. The risen life of Christ through the gifts of his Spirit can then suggest what is to be done or not done in incredible detail.

This state of consciousness is not passing, but a permanent awareness that spontaneously envelops the whole of life. The X-ray eyes of faith, which penetrate through outward appearances, perceive all things in God and God in all things. Thus the movement from the takeoff point of sacred symbol to spiritual attentiveness, to ever-deepening absorption of the faculties in God, and to the purification of the unconscious terminates in the transforming union. The latter involves a restructuring of consciousness that perceives a new dimension to all reality. We live without the consoling spiritual experiences of the past, but with the mature awareness of a purified faith and love that is open to the divine energy of grace directly and continuously.

Whatever we experience of God, however exalted, is only a radiance of his presence. No experience in this life can be God as he is in himself because God infinitely transcends all categories and experiences. In the transforming union, the energy of faith, trust, and love is constantly being beamed to us whether we experience it or not. The body has been prepared and stabilized by the practice of virtue and the purification of sense and spirit so that it can receive the divine communications uninterruptedly. Divine love can now manifest itself in all our activities, even the most ordinary. The same all-pervasive union is present while walking down the street or brushing one's teeth as in periods of contemplative prayer. External and internal realities are unified because all are equally rooted in God and manifest God. The entire organism is sensitized to all the ways in which the divine presence manifests itself, without mistaking any one of them as the ultimate expression of God's love.

The divine energy in itself is infinite potentiality and actuality. Creatures are localized manifestations of it. If there is no obstacle in us, no false self, we become spiritual transmitters through whom the divine presence as boundless love and compassion communicates itself to others in ever-widening circles of influence.

Transforming union is the ripe fruit of dismantling the false self. As soon as the false self is reduced to zero, transforming union occurs. A nonpossessive attitude toward everything, including ourselves, is established because there is no longer a self-centered "I" to possess anything. That does not mean that we do not use the good things of life, but now they are not ends in themselves but stepping-stones to God's presence. The Spirit's energy filters down from the still point into all the other faculties, purifying the external senses so that they can perceive God's presence and action in every sense experience. What is true, beautiful, and good in everything that exists becomes transparent.

Transforming union can be manifested in various ways: patience in illness and external trials, as in Job; intense solitude, as in the case of Anthony; demanding ministries. But it has to express itself in a more than ordinary way because the energy for good that divine union releases is tremendous. From particle physics we have a description of what occurs when a particle returns to the wave pattern from which it came. The power of the wave is far greater than the localized particle. It was from his movement into the very heart of the divine love that Anthony drew his strength.

We may think of God as the Heavenly King dominating all creation, and of course he is in charge of everything. Notice, however, that he exercises that authority by serving creation all the time. He created and nurtures this planet with exquisite care, providing air, water, food, and all kinds of natural resources, all day long. Service without seeking any return characterizes the Ultimate Reality. Those in transforming union are beginning to find that out. Hence, they too become servants, not dominators.

Transforming union is the goal of the first part of the Christian spiritual journey. Despite its rarity, it should be regarded as the normal Christian life. We must then translate all our relationships —with God, ourselves, other people, and the cosmos—into this new perspective and way of being in the world. The principal means of reaching transforming union is the personal love of Christ.

The next part of the journey is to learn the meaning of Jesus' words, "The Father and I are one" (John 10:30), and the consequences of his prayer, "That they may be one in us" (John 17:21).

18

The First Four Beatitudes

The beatitudes are the quintessence of the teaching of Jesus. They represent his comprehensive approach to happiness. They are the outpouring of the Spirit in the Pentecostal grace. We have within us, by virtue of baptism, the seven gifts of the Spirit: reverence, piety, knowledge, fortitude, counsel, understanding, and wisdom. These gifts are activated by dismantling the straitjacket of the false self so that the communication of the divine light and love may be received with ever-increasing clarity and fullness.

The beatitudes are wisdom sayings that express the disposition appropriate to each level of consciousness. They highlight both the goodness and the limitations of each stage of development. The object of the spiritual journey is the healing of body, mind, and spirit. Jesus said, "The healthy do not need a doctor; sick people do. I have not come to invite the self-righteous to a change of heart, but sinners" (Luke 5:31–33). A physician does not heal people by killing them. Similarly, the Spirit does not heal the wounds of early childhood and the emotional programs for happiness by destroying the instincts that gave rise to them. Rather, whatever was good in the instinctual needs must be preserved and integrated into the unfolding values of the human organism. The biological need for survival is essential to keep going in this world when the going gets tough; only the exaggerations and distortions of these instinctual needs are left behind. The grace of the Spirit heals each level of consciousness in order to enable the values proper to each level to contribute to the wholeness of the human organism with all its potentialities.

The first beatitude addresses the level of consciousness that we experienced in coming into the world, the reptilian consciousness, in which there is no awareness of a separate self. The principal focus of reptilian consciousness is food, shelter, survival, and the prompt fulfillment of physical needs. Privations during this period of childhood may later give rise to drives to possess the symbols of security in the culture. "How happy you would be," Jesus says, "if you were poor in spirit," that is, if you put your trust in God rather than in possessions or other symbols of security.

The poor in spirit are those who accept afflictions for God's sake. They are not only the materially poor, but also those who suffer any affliction, whether emotional, mental, or physical, and who accept their situation out of love of God. The poor have a special claim on the kingdom because they literally do not have anything, or if they do have possessions, they are willing to let them go as the needs of others or the will of God may require. The gift of the Spirit called "reverence" empowers the poor to place their trust in God rather than in the symbols of security that the culture provides.

The experience of happiness in the face of destitution, poverty, and affliction is the fruit of accepting what is. By accepting reality, we are free of our predetermined demands and "shoulds." It is not just a passive acceptance, however. We may also be asked by God to do something to change, improve, or correct situations, including defending ourselves or others when circumstances call for it.

The part-human, part-animal typhonic consciousness characteristic of the emotional life of the child is addressed by the second and third beatitudes. At this level of consciousness, the drive for affection/esteem and pleasure and the drive for power and control may turn these instinctual needs into centers of motivation that dominate our lives.

The second beatitude "Happy are those who mourn, for they will be comforted" speaks to the exaggerated demand for affection/esteem and pleasure. The refusal to let go of what is being taken from us creates tension. When we let go of some person, place, or thing that we love, we automatically enter a period of mourning. If we accept the loss of what we loved, we experience freedom from what we formerly depended upon excessively and we enter into a new relationship with it, based on the new freedom that does not try to squeeze absolute happiness from passing pleasures. If we pursue particular pleasures in the name of happiness, we make them into idols.

The third beatitude, "Happy are the meek," addresses the drive for power, as if to say, "How happy you would be if you did not want to control situations, other people, or your own life, and if you possessed the freedom to accept insults and injustice without being blown away."

Each one of the three emotional programs develops in the context of a self-consciousness that is increasing without the reassurance of divine union. Each time we move to a further level of self-consciousness, the separate-self sense is enhanced, and we experience a heightened feeling of alienation.

Christian tradition has suggested various disciplines to initiate the healing of the reptilian level of consciousness. As infants we were engrossed by our physical needs: eating, sleeping, being caressed, and having our bodily needs promptly serviced. By deliberately upsetting our habits of eating, sleeping, and daily living through fasting, vigils, and simplifying our lifestyle, we create a space in which to change. A situation of temporary privation can alert us to the fact that we are not as dependent on physical demands as we had thought. Bodily discipline, work in the service of the community, and manual labor develop control over physical impulses. Through such practices we can reduce our overdependency on the prompt fulfillment of our desires for pleasure.

The traditional means of overcoming the drive to control others is the practice of fraternal charity, accepting people as they are without trying to change them, and the service of others through the corporal and spiritual works of mercy: feeding the hungry, visiting the sick and those in prison, and responding to the various forms of physical, mental, and spiritual needs.

Our efforts to practice the dismantling of the emotional programs for happiness and to serve the needs of others attract the movement of the Spirit. It is in response to our efforts that God's passive purifications come to our assistance and take us far beyond anything that we could do alone to free the reptilian and typhonic levels of consciousness from their respective hang-ups.

The mythic membership level of consciousness brings our programs for happiness into contact with the social development that took place from four to eight years of age, during which time we absorbed the value systems of parents, teachers, peer groups, and television programs. A child does not have the use of reason to evaluate these influences, so he or she absorbs them unquestioningly, and relates his or her emotional programs for happiness to the new social situation. The emotional programs we created to cope with the difficult situations of infancy are now extended into the vast world of social relationships, making those programs far more complex.

The fourth beatitude "Happy are those who hunger and thirst for justice; they will have their fill" addresses overidentification with our social group and frees us from the urgency to be accepted and approved by the group. In order to respond to the invitation of the gospel, we need to go beyond the behavior that may be held in honor or demanded by the particular social group to which we belong. This does not mean that we should reject our country, religion, ethnic roots, or families. While remaining grateful for the good things we have received and loyal to family and social group, we recognize that such loyalty is not an absolute. We try to improve unhealthy or unjust situations in our family or community instead of clinging to a naive loyalty that refuses to see defects or fails to suggest improvements or corrections that should be made. We have the freedom to remain within our tradition or institution, while at the same time working for its renewal. We do what we can to improve family, church, or social situations without demanding results or expecting to see the fruits of our labors. The Spirit gives us courage to make our personal response to Christ, rather than one that is based on what others say, do, or expect.

The beatitudes are directed to the growth of inner freedom. Progress toward inner freedom depends on the firmness of our commitment. The gift of fortitude is reflected in the beatitude "Happy are the meek for they shall inherit the earth." The meek are those who do not want to control anybody or to push other people around, and who are willing to be insulted and set aside without being unduly upset by such opposition. They do not draw their identity from what other people say or think, but from the values of the gospel. The fortitude that belongs to the meek is the fortitude that stands firm in the face of opposition, as Anthony did in the tombs. Thomas Aquinas says that having the patience to hold one's ground requires greater courage than fighting back.

This leads to a deeper understanding of the passion of Christ, learned from our own personal struggles with life and not just from an abstract reading of the gospels.

The beatitudes are an invitation to assimilate the values proclaimed by Jesus. We struggle with the difficulties of life, depending
on him and believing in his help, without demanding to feel consolation or depending on it. The first four beatitudes correspond to
the commandment, "Love your neighbor as yourself." They enable
us to graduate from our childish programs once and for all and to
move into the freedom to which Jesus invites us. They prepare us for
the continuing work of letting go of selfishness and of sensitizing
ourselves to the movements of the Spirit, which invite us not only to
generous efforts, but also to heroic service of God and other people.

19

The Last Four Beatitudes

"Happy are the merciful, mercy will be shown to them" is the fifth beatitude and corresponds to the full reflective self-consciousness of mental egoic consciousness. At this level we become fully human. Our response to life is cooperative, nonjudgmental, and accepting of others. This beatitude fulfills Christ's new commandment, "Love one another as I have loved you" (John 15:12).

The new commandment is much more demanding than the commandment to love one's neighbor as oneself. To love one's neighbor as oneself is to respect the image of God in our neighbor with all the rights which that dignity confers. To love one another as Jesus loves us is to love one another in our humanness—in our individuality and opinionatedness, in personality conflicts and in unbearable situations. It is to continue to show love, no matter what the provocation may be to act otherwise.

The merciful are those whose concern is beginning to expand beyond family and loved ones into the larger community. Their concern ultimately includes the whole human family, past, present, and to come. The ultimate goal of Jesus is to engage us in the redemption of the world. The beatitudes impart the steadfast love of God who makes the sun to shine on the good and the not-so-good, on those who respond and on those who do not respond.

In our time an important aspect of the beatitude of the merciful is to practice compassion toward ourselves. Many people come to self-consciousness with a low self-image and suffer from varying degrees of self-hatred. This disposition is pride in reverse. Instead of reaching out for self-aggrandizement, these people demean themselves because they do not measure up to the idealized image of perfection that their self-image demands. When they fail to meet this impossible standard, pride, not God, says, "You're no good!" They then feel shame for failing to measure up to the grandiose expectations of themselves that their upbringing, culture, or drive to overachieve created.

Most of us have a heavy burden of emotional junk accumulated from early childhood. The body serves as the storehouse for this undigested emotional material. The Spirit initiates the process of healing by evacuating the junk. This takes place as a result of the deep rest of mind and body in centering prayer. The energy formerly used up in trying to cope with current emotional stress is now available for growth. The straitjacket of the false self squeezes people into an infinitesimal use of their human potentialities. The beatitudes enable them to expand and to start to access these immense possibilities.

As prayer becomes more intimate, grace reaches down into the depths of our psyche, empowering it to unload the emotional damage and debris of a lifetime. In time we will make the transition from going to God through reason and particular acts of the will to going to him more directly through the intuitive faculties. Then God will relate to us through them instead of through the external senses, memory, imagination, reasoning, and acts of the will. This period of transition may be experienced as a crisis of faith. We are moving from the mental egoic to the intuitive level of consciousness.

Once the intuitive level is established, all our relationships change—toward ourselves, God, other people, and the cosmos—and we spend a significant period of time adjusting to this new way of being in the world.

The beatitude that corresponds to the intuitive level is the sixth beatitude which is the pure of heart and the promise is, "They will see God." They will see him not with their bodily eyes, of course, but with the eyes of the spirit purified by faith.

Purified in the night of sense, faith penetrates beyond appearances to the hidden reality. Rituals, sacraments, nature, art, friendship, and the service of others become transparent, and we access the Mystery that is manifesting itself through each of these symbols or events. Everything begins to speak to us of God. Happiness arises from the perception of God's closeness and our sense of belonging to the universe. The feeling of closeness may be manifested in spiritual experiences such as the stages of "felt" contemplation, as we saw in chapter thirteen. Such experiences may deepen through ever-increasing absorption in God during prayer, and alert us to his presence in daily life, events, and other people.

Having experienced the beatitude of seeing God in ourselves and others, we come to the crisis of trust called the night of spirit, during which the longing for divine union becomes acute. This is the level to which the seventh beatitude of the peacemakers is addressed. Peace, according to the classical definition of Augustine, is the tranquility of order. The right order of human nature consists in the effective integration of our emotional and rational lives into our intuitive faculties and the surrender of our unified nature to God in love. In divine union, the great "I" of Jesus Christ becomes our "I." Our identity becomes rooted in him rather than in our own interests. If we still have interests, we are ready to give them up at the request of the Spirit, who has become the senior partner, so to speak, of the firm.

Peace is the great gift of Jesus to his apostles on the day of his resurrection. The peace that Jesus offers is not sentimental. This peace
transcends joy and sorrow, hope and despair. This peace is rooted in
a way of being that transcends the emotions. We are no longer blown
away by the winds of persecution, nor washed away by the floods
of tribulation. Our house is built on rock, and the rock is Christ.
That rock is strength against every storm. Divine union has become
an invincible conviction, a way of being, a fourth dimension to all
reality.

Entering into union with God makes one God-like, which is quite
different from becoming God. At times spiritual consolation in the
states prior to the night of spirit are so fantastic that one feels "as
if one were God." John of the Cross says such experiences can be
even stronger after the transforming union. However, the tendency
of the transforming union as an abiding state is rather to be without
extraordinary experiences and to lead ordinary daily life in an unob-
trusive way. If one has special gifts, these are exercised in dependence
on God. One is completely free of the results and does not draw one's
identity from any glamorous role, but is simply, like God, the servant
of creation.

The eighth beatitude belongs to a further stage of consciousness,
the stage of perfect wisdom. "Blessed are those who are persecuted
because of righteousness for theirs is the kingdom of heaven." This
is the wisdom that finds happiness in persecution. "Be happy," Jesus
says in effect, "if people say the worst things they can about you, or
when you suffer for the truth, for justice, or for my name. Rejoice.
Dance for joy for your reward is very great in heaven." In this extraordinary world view, persecution endured for God is the peak of happiness. Those who have experienced this beatitude have moved beyond
self-interest to such a degree that they no longer have a possessive
attitude toward themselves. Their identity is rooted in Christ and the

unique identity he wants them to have. If their vocation requires suffering, they perceive that they are then serving him more effectively. They not only enter into the peace of Christ but also become sources of the divine life and peace for others. The graced energy received from God, like an ever-flowing stream, is shared with those with whom they live and far beyond. Through them, God is pouring the divine light, life, and love into the human family.

20

The Essence of Centering Prayer

L et us begin by clarifying what contemplation is not, in order to better understand what it is. Contemplative prayer is not a technique, although it makes use of methods as starting points to awaken spiritual attentiveness. It is not a magic carpet to bliss, a spiritual happy hour, a respectable substitute for mind-changing drugs, self-hypnosis, or a trance state.

Contemplative prayer should not be identified with charismatic gifts. These are enumerated by Paul (1 Cor. 12:7–11): speaking in various languages, interpreting the languages, speaking with knowledge, healing, performing miracles, speaking with wisdom, preaching, discerning spirits, administering, and others. All the charisms, according to Paul, are aimed at encouraging the local Christian community. Their primary purpose is not to benefit or sanctify the one who has them. These gifts do not necessarily indicate either the presence of contemplative prayer or holiness. Hence, our admiration for them should be measured.

Perhaps the most striking of the charisms is resting in the Spirit, formerly called "slaying in the Spirit." It is communicated by an anointing or blessing, or simply by the glance of the healer. Those who receive this gift experience the attraction to rest in God. They may resist or consent. If they consent, their external senses are slightly suspended and they sink to the floor. There is the human tendency, because the experience is so delightful, to want to prolong it by staying on the floor or by going back to the healer for more. It is important in our day, when charismatic gifts are multiplying, that a well-balanced teaching be offered to help people understand the true value of these particular gifts. They are an invitation to begin the spiritual journey, not an invitation to be blissed out as often as possible. The latter is spiritual gluttony.

Many people receive occasional mystical graces that are significant and sometimes very powerful. Since God is present within us, he may reach up and pull us down anytime, or let a wisp of the delicious perfume of his presence escape from his secret place within us. Even people who are not especially religious may have this kind of experience. Ordinary Christian instruction in our time does not usually articulate Christian mystical experience, so when these experiences arise spontaneously, most average Christians cannot understand them or articulate them. We may even be frightened by them. Actually these graces are gilt-edged invitations. Christ is saying, "Follow me"—not in words but through the experience. If we want just to lie on the floor, we might as well take a nap.

Another kind of experience, often mistaken for contemplative prayer, is the realm of psychic gifts or parapsychological phenomena. These are multiplying so much in our time that some anthropologists believe that the human family as a whole is moving from the mental egoic to the intuitive level of consciousness. We are beginning to grasp the fact that the human brain possesses potentialities not commonly tapped or explored, which are simply by-products of the process of human growth. If this energy were well grounded in the body by means of chanting, Taoist or yogic exercises, vigorous walking, moderate jogging, or light work like crafts or gardening, the body itself would normally distribute the increase of energy. If the natural energy gets stuck in the body or nervous system, however, it may manifest itself in psychic or physical phenomena.

The false self is still at work on the intuitive level of consciousness. What the intuitive level provides—and it is a significant growth of the human potential—is new energy. But energy is only energy; it is how we use it that matters. As we have seen, spiritual energies can be used for self-aggrandizement and the domination of people who may be fascinated by unusual gifts. Both charismatic gifts and psychic powers can easily go to one's head if the false self has not first been purified in some significant degree. The night of spirit is a necessary corrective before one can exercise these gifts without the danger of spiritual pride turning it into some form of self-exaltation.

Let us now look at mystical phenomena. These are psychic phenomena that are inspired by the divine presence and action, such as bodily ecstasies, locutions (words spoken externally, in the imagination, or in the spirit), and external or internal visions. The apparitions of Lourdes and Fatima, insofar as they are authentic, are probably charisms designed to encourage the Christian people in times of disaster, war, and persecution. They are a call to repentance and prayer.

In the Hindu tradition, there are over a hundred *siddhis* or psychic powers listed by Patanjali, a near contemporary of Jesus. These powers are meant to be integrated into the unfolding levels of consciousness. If one gets stuck at any stage, however spiritual, and does not continue to grow, the gifts proper to that stage may stagnate. Special gifts that started out as very beneficial can then become harmful, both for oneself if one falls into spiritual pride, and for others if one tries to exploit them for the sake of personal gratification.

One of the great levitators of all time was Saint Joseph of Cupertino, a seventeenth-century Capuchin. At a certain period in his spiritual development, Joseph was experiencing the exuberant mysticism we described earlier. He was so much in love with God that when he heard the name of Jesus he would frequently rise into the air. He sometimes rose not just a few feet like most levitators, but right up to the ceiling. For the friars trying to chant the divine office in choir, this became a problem. The superiors began to take a dim view of Joseph's gift. However, he was such an exemplary religious that they remained silent and waited to see what might develop. One day a huge cross weighing half a ton arrived at the monastery to be set in place on top of the church steeple. Derricks had not been invented, and the scaffolding was found to be defective. It was too dangerous to lug the cross to the top of the steeple. While the friars stood around wringing their hands, Joseph felt inspired by the Spirit to do the job. Letting out a little cry as he lifted off, he grabbed the huge cross, flew to the top of the steeple, and set it in place. Then he gently descended to earth. It is also recorded that when Joseph was talking with other friars and the name of Jesus was mentioned, his heart would at times be so smitten by divine love that he would interiorly melt into God. Without realizing what he was doing, he would grab the other friar and they both would rise. This was too much for the superiors. They ordered Joseph to stop levitating. He indicated that it was not in his power to resist this upward movement when it came over him, but they insisted. Since he was a very obedient religious, he kept trying to resist the upward urge. We are told that Joseph went into a "depression." Was this a euphemism for the night of spirit which sometimes manifests similar symptoms? If so, it was the experience of the night of spirit that transformed him, not levitation.

Parapsychological phenomena are only by-products of contemplation, not the essence of it. No manufacturer goes into business for the sake of by-products. If we give psychic or spiritual byproducts too much emphasis, we are making a mistake; they can even become a hindrance to the spiritual journey if we have a conscious or unconscious attachment to them. It is only after the night of spirit has done its work that the secret satisfaction of being a specially chosen soul is finally reduced to zero.

In our time, spiritual guides are needed who are thoroughly familiar with the Christian contemplative tradition, the stages of prayer, and the traps along the way, so that they can encourage people who are entering the dark nights of sense. The number of such people is constantly increasing. They need the guidance that can come only from someone who has already had some experience of contemplative prayer. They need the warnings that come from spiritual wisdom about not making too much of psychic or mystical phenomena. One cannot live on the frosting of a cake; one needs the solid food of pure faith.

21

A Pure Faith

The essence of contemplative prayer is not the way of external or internal phenomena, but the way of pure faith. This is the narrow door that leads to life.

The tendency to identify contemplative prayer with felt experience is very deeply ingrained in us, however—and, unfortunately, it keeps getting reinforced. There has been a tendency among spiritual writers in recent centuries to identify contemplation with the felt presence of God or the unfolding of the spiritual senses—the sensation, in prayer, of experiencing God's presence within as directly as experiencing the objects of the senses of smell, touch, and taste. In textbooks dealing with spiritual theology, we find the assumption, either stated or presupposed, that contemplation must be felt to be real.

Many persons on the contemplative path, including cloistered religious, are committed to the practice of contemplative prayer and yet have never experienced the inflow of divine grace according to the pattern laid out by Teresa of Avila and other mystics. But does that make them any less contemplatives? Ruth Burrows in her book *Guidelines for Mystical Prayer*[1] describes two nuns whom she knew intimately. One was a sister in a Carmelite convent; the other was an active religious with a busy and hectic ministry in the world. The active sister was the exuberant mystic. The other sister was the typical plodding, faithful, obedient religious who practiced contemplative prayer day after day for thirty or forty years, experiencing it most of the time as drudgery, boredom, and an endless bombardment of unwanted thoughts. Instead of coming out of the night of sense, she either remained in it or went into the night of spirit without any transition. Ruth Burrows says both of these nuns arrived at transforming union at about the same time.

Teresa of Avila suggested once in her writings that the prayer of full union might be a short cut to transforming union. That may indeed be its purpose. It may be a special way of hastening the ordinary process of dismantling the false self. Ruth Burrows extrapolates that exuberant mysticism may be a charism. Some persons are given the necessary psychological experience in order to explain the various stages of contemplation for the benefit of the majority of contemplatives who are led by the hidden ladder described by John of the Cross.

This brings us to the remarkable insight of John of the Cross that contemplative prayer is fundamentally a ray of darkness. Again and again he identifies pure faith as the proximate means of union with God. Hence, any experience of the divine that we may enjoy is not God, but our interpretation of God, or the radiance of God's action in us. Pure faith transcends every human experience and accesses God just as God is. If a ray of light passed through a perfect vacuum, John of the Cross writes, we would have no knowledge of it, because in a perfect vacuum there are no dust particles to reflect the physical energy as light. When we accept it as it is, the divine light is constantly beaming into our whole being—body, soul, and spirit. Even the spiritual senses do not access the immense purity and power of the divine energy in its essence.

In this life it is not possible to see God just as God is and live, according to the author of the First Epistle of John. But we can consent to know him in the darkness of faith, and in that darkness the invincible conviction of the divine presence arises. If we could grasp this basic insight of John of the Cross, it would free us from an immense amount of anxiety in the journey. Most of our troubles come from expectations that are unrealistic and cannot be fulfilled.

The narrow way of pure faith leads to life. This teaching of John of the Cross might be exemplified by reflecting on the difference between taking an express elevator to the top floor of a skyscraper and taking a local. The local elevator stops at every floor, and at every stop the vista gets better. The problem is that one may never get back on the elevator because one is so entranced by the view. John of the Cross forbids his disciples to accept psychic phenomena or to desire substantial touches. "The latter," he acknowledges, "are part of divine union and can be accepted, but not desired." As for locutions, sweet odors, or visions coming from outside or from within, he strongly recommends resisting them.

The higher the gifts, the more we need the nights of sense and spirit to protect us from the residue of the false self and spiritual pride. If we get hooked on spiritual pride, progress on the journey comes to a screeching halt. The wisdom of taking the express elevator— the way of pure faith—to the top floor is that it avoids all mystical phenomena that might occur as by-products of the unloading of the unconscious. The way of pure faith is to persevere in contemplative practice without worrying about where we are on the journey, and without comparing ourselves with others or judging others' gifts as better than ours. We can be spared all this nonsense if we surrender ourselves to the divine action, whatever the psychological content of our prayer may be. In pure faith, the results are often hidden even from those who are growing the most.

Let us return to the story of the nun who affirmed that she never had any experience of the inflowing of mystical (felt) grace. She persevered in contemplative prayer when it was dull and routine, enduring severe struggles with her primitive feelings and the unloading of emotional trauma from early childhood. One day she was walking in the convent garden when suddenly she was aware that everything had changed. The "I" of her ego-identity was reduced to nothing, and the big "I AM" of Christ had moved to center stage in her awareness. The source of her identity was no longer the self that she had known, but Christ's presence within her. The risen life of Christ began manifesting itself in everything she did, sleeping or waking, and communicating to her the strength to fulfill her vocation with unwearying determination.

Thus it is commitment to the journey and fidelity to the practice that leads to transforming union, not spiritual experiences. Such experiences, of course, may help to bring us to this commitment. Sometimes we need them in order to heal the wounds and the emotional pain of childhood. But once our emotions have been healed, God gets down to business and begins to treat us like adults. Then we are initiated into the narrow path that leads to life, which is the way of pure faith.

The divine light of faith is totally available in the degree that we consent and surrender ourselves to its presence and action within us. It heals the wounds of a lifetime and brings us to transforming union, empowering us to enter Christ's redemptive program, first by the healing of our own deep wounds, and then by sharing in the healing of others.

If the divine energy of grace is penetrating our being to the roots at every moment, it is bound to have effects in our lives. Persons in transforming union manifest who they are by how they live. But the chances are good that they themselves will not perceive this. Lay people living quiet, prayerful lives in the world, who think they are not contemplatives because they never became monks or nuns, and elderly religious, who think they are not contemplatives because of the misunderstandings about contemplative prayer in recent centuries, may be so holy that they are not even upset by their apparent failure as contemplatives. This is the triumph of hiddenness.

22

From Contemplation to Action

Afew years ago a motion picture appeared called *The Mission*. It dealt with a historical situation that existed in the seventeenth century in South America near the borders of what are now Paraguay, Argentina, and Brazil. Jesuit missionaries had created a community in which the natives were becoming self-supporting. These indigenous people had been for many years the prey of political forces in Europe vying for control of their land. The success of the Jesuit missionaries in raising them to a certain well-being and autonomy was threatening the slave trade in the area and the extension of the colonial aspirations of Spain and Portugal.

The Spanish and Portuguese governments were putting enormous pressure on Church authorities to end this mission so that the dwindling slave trade could be expanded without the opposition of the missionaries and the developing native community. The Spanish and Portuguese agents threatened to close all Jesuit institutions in their respective countries if the Holy See did not close the mission. The Apostolic Visitor, a former Jesuit, arrived on the scene with secret instructions from the Holy See to close the mission in order to save the Jesuit institutions in Europe and throughout the world. To understand the dilemma in which this man was placed, we have to keep in mind that the Jesuits were introducing the reforms of the Council of Trent and establishing colleges, retreat houses, and missions all over the world. To close down all these efforts for the renewal of the Church would have been a serious loss and even a disaster.

As the movie progresses the Apostolic Visitor witnesses the remarkable work that the local Jesuits are doing at the mission. He meets the happy and industrious native people who have come out of the jungle and received the enlightened social teaching of the Jesuit missionaries along with the Christian faith. After an agonizing interior struggle and much prayer, he gives the order to close the mission. The natives refuse to leave. Several of the Jesuit missionaries side with them, while the founder of the mission refuses to resort to violence to defend it.

Mercenaries are hired by the European powers; they attack the helpless mission with cannons and massacre all the natives and the missionaries. In the last scene, the ambassadors of Spain and Portugal meet with the Apostolic Visitor to report what has happened. The Visitor is appalled by the extent of the massacre. "Was this massacre really necessary?" he demands with mounting indignation. One of the ambassadors, seeking to calm the Visitor's rage and horror, answers soothingly, "Your Eminence, do not feel badly. After all, such is the way the world is!"

The Visitor replies, "No! . . . Such is the way *we* have made the world!" Rising from his chair, he walks to the window, fixes his gaze on something outside, and, as if speaking to himself, adds a further precision, "Such is the way *I* have made the world!" There is the glimmer of a tear in one of his eyes.

The plot of *The Mission* focuses on the most crucial question of our time and one that is addressed to each of us. It is the question of responsibility for social injustice. What happens when the rights of the innocent interfere with the economic or territorial interests of world powers? At the mythic membership level of consciousness, the response is, "Such is the way the world is." Whoever has the most money or power wins. The national interest always comes first. The mature Christian conscience says, "No! This is unjust! The exploitation of the innocent by armed force cannot be tolerated. Oppression is a collective sin of enormous magnitude and carries with it the most serious consequences. How can I free myself from being implicated in so great an evil?"

The limitations of mythic membership consciousness, especially its naive loyalty to the values of a particular cultural or interest group, hinder us from fully responding to the values of the gospel. We bring to personal and social problems the prepackaged values and preconceived ideas that are deeply ingrained in us. The beatitude that hungers and thirsts for justice urges us to take personal responsibility for our attitudes to God, other people, the ecology of the earth, and the vast and worsening social problems of our time.

Abraham Lincoln, influenced by the cultural conditioning of his time, hesitated to sign the Emancipation Proclamation. In the first months of his administration, his primary consideration was to preserve the union. Since the Constitution provided for states' rights and slavery in the South was such a right, he favored allowing the South to maintain slavery as long as the practice was not extended to the new territories opening up in the west. It was only with time that he saw that the evil of slavery was the primary issue of the Civil War and issued the Emancipation Proclamation.

The Christian denominations sent missionaries into Asia with a chip on their shoulders, which was the colonial mentality of Europe. The missionaries preached from the viewpoint that Western culture was better than Eastern, and that the people of Asia were a bunch of pagans. Actually, the Asians in many instances had a higher culture than the medieval barbarians the Church had been trying for centuries to convert in Europe. The mindset of the missionaries did not allow them to question their preconceptions and prepackaged values. As a result, they made virtually no inroads in Asia in four centuries of evangelization. Since they had no appreciation of the local culture, it did not occur to them to try to live the gospel from inside the culture.

In our time, Abbe Monchanin, Henri LeSaux, and Father Bede Griffiths have pioneered the latter approach in India. In Father Griffiths's ashram, texts from the Hindu scriptures are incorporated into the liturgy along with the customs of the *sannyasi*, the monastics of India. The values of Christian monastic life are lived in terms that the local people can understand. That is the genius of those who are free to use their creativity in the service of God and who have graduated from excessive dependence on their early religious education and the philosophical or nationalistic values of the secular culture.

Would the Catholic population in general have acquiesced so easily to the Nazi regime if they had graduated from the mythical membership level of consciousness and had taken personal responsibility for their relationship to the Nazi movement? Franz Jagerstetter refused to be drafted into the German army because he believed that the war was unjust. He had a family he loved, but that was not his highest priority. His conscience said, "You cannot support this unjust regime or its war!" He refused to join the German army, was put into jail, and eventually was beheaded. It is because he is a martyr to conscience that he is a martyr to religion.

The seventh beatitude is "Blessed are the peacemakers." Jesus did not say, "Blessed are the peace-lovers." The latter are people who do not want to rock the boat and hence sweep embarrassing situations under the rug. Capitalistic systems are embarrassed by the homeless and try to hide them. Communist regimes were embarrassed by dissidents and tried to hide them. Every mindset, bias, and prejudice is afraid of peacemakers. Authorities can deal with the peace-lovers by appealing to their desire not to have their lives upset by the oppression and misery of other people. Mythic membership mindsets lead to serious injustices because they tend to disregard the rights and needs of others.

The movement beyond mythical membership consciousness is essential to becoming fully human. Although humanity as a whole began to access the mental egoic level of consciousness around 3000 B.C.E., its mature vision of personal responsibility still has to be interiorized by each of us. Such maturity is vigorously opposed by the downward pull of regressive tendencies and overidentification with national, ethnic, tribal, and religious groups from which we draw our sense of belonging and self-worth. These regressive tendencies hinder us from taking responsibility for the injustices that are perpetuated in the name of our particular community.

Nations still try to solve their differences from a mythic membership level of consciousness, as the following analogy may illustrate. Here is a youngster of four or five playing with a friend in a sandbox. He suddenly gets the idea that he would like to have the sandbox all to himself. He says to his friend, "Get out of my sandbox." The other replies, "I will not"—"Yes you will"—"I will not"—"Yes you will." Finally, the boy shoves his former friend out of the sandbox. This is so much fun that he goes to all the other sandboxes on the beach and punches one child after another until they all get out of their sandboxes. Now he has ten sandboxes, a domain—an empire!

This approach to disagreements among nations is manifestly irrational, especially when weapons have become so destructive that those who use them against an enemy are likely to destroy themselves. One of the basic requirements of the Just War Theory is not to injure or kill the innocent. Given the weaponry that is available, this essential condition is now absolutely impossible. The wars of our century have destroyed many times more civilians than soldiers, and the proportion goes on increasing.

One wonders what the responsibility of the world religions is in this situation. Historically they have contributed to serious violence, war, prejudice, bigotry, and endless division. Yet more than any other institution, they have an obligation to address the problem of world peace and to emphasize the human values that they mutually share and proclaim. Their collective conscience could challenge the nationalistic interests of world powers. But as yet they have no networking process or place where they might speak with one voice on behalf of basic human values, especially justice and peace. We cannot expect the military establishment to end war. War is their profession. The only way that war can be eliminated is to make it socially unacceptable. If the world religions would speak to the human family regarding its common source and the potential of every human being to be transformed into the divine, a moral voice of great power would be introduced on behalf of the innocent and of the human family as a whole.

One cannot be a Christian without social concern. There is no reason why anyone should go hungry even for a day. Since the resources are there, why do millions continue to starve? The answer must be greed. It is, for most people, an unconscious greed stemming from a mindset that does not ask the right questions and a world view that is out of date. Those who have reached the mental egoic consciousness perceive the necessity to be persons of dialogue, harmony, cooperation, forgiveness, and compassion. The problems of our time have to be dealt with creatively—from the inner freedom to rethink ethical principles in light of the globalization of world society now taking place.

One of these problems is our relationship to the earth of which we are stewards. At the very least, we have the obligation to pass on the environment intact to the next generation. We are only brief sojourners on this planet and must consider what happens after we are gone. When we pass on, we will obviously have a new relationship to the human family, but our attitude toward it while we were alive will continue after death. That is the meaning of the parable of the Last Judgment (Matt. 25:31–46). Our humanity in some form is not going to disappear after death. What we do, or fail to do, to the least of God's little ones is going to happen to us in eternity.

In his parable Jesus identifies those who will receive the kingdom of God: "I was sick and you visited me, hungry and you fed me, in prison and you came to me" (Matt. 25:35). According to these words, Christ suffers in the needy and the afflicted. Insofar as we access the mind of Christ, we too identify with the sufferings of others and reach out to help according to our possibilities.

The realization of Christ suffering in the oppressed is the fruit of intuitive consciousness which brings to full growth the seeds sown during the mental egoic period. The average level of consciousness of people today has yet to graduate from mythic membership into the maturity of mental egoic consciousness. The contemplative journey, of its very nature, calls us forth to act in a fully human way under the inspiration of the gifts of the Spirit. These gifts provide the divine energy of grace not only to accept what is, but also to change what is unjust. The gift of fortitude creates the hunger and thirst for justice. This disposition frees us from the downward pull of regressive tendencies and from the undue influence of cultural conditioning. As in the case of Anthony, it frees us from all fear.

The human family is still immersed in the patriarchal culture that arose around 3000 B.C.E. By no stretch of the imagination can we affirm that men and women are treated equally in the present cultures of the world. This inequality is greater in some cultures than in others, depending on where a particular culture is on the scale of the evolutionary process. Only an institutional commitment to the beatitudes can offset the institutional commitment to exploitation characteristic of addictive societies. The Second Vatican Council was a movement of the Spirit to make the values of the gospel available to everyone on earth. That requires translating its message into terms that people can understand through structures adapted to mental egoic consciousness and providing practical examples of concern without which words are useless.

A delicate shift seems to be taking place in the Christian consciousness since World War II. The ideal of Nazareth—simplicity of lifestyle, the domestic virtues, unquestioning obedience to authority—has been the basic model of Christian holiness since the end of the age of martyrdom in the fourth century. With the movement of humanity as a whole toward mental egoic and intuitive consciousness, this model of holiness is changing. The will of God in important matters can no longer be discerned by simple obedience alone. Other factors have to be taken into account as well, such as the actual circumstances, expert advice, the needs of others, the interior attraction of grace, spiritual direction, and the signs of the times. Mental egoic consciousness urges us to assume personal responsibility for our response to Christ in every situation. It does not limit itself to the conventional morality of a local parish, diocese, or religious community. It feels responsible for the whole Church and for the entire human family. Its respect for authority and tradition is genuine, but its sense of responsibility impels it to initiate ways of making the challenges of the gospel better known and available, especially the contemplative dimension and the social implications.

23

Contemplation in Action

Archbishop Dom Helder Camara started what are called the "base communities" in South and Central America. These communities teach people to take responsibility both as individuals and as communities for their response to the gospel. This may mean taking political stances since the policies of certain governments are manifestly unjust. The members of base communities read the gospel as if they were part of it, identifying themselves with the characters in the text, and applying the gospel principles in their daily lives. To my knowledge, this is the first time that groups of people have addressed the question: "Can we live the beatitudes not only as individuals, but also as a community?" If there were institutions with such a Magna Carta, they would change the world.

I had the privilege of introducing Dom Helder at a meeting of World Religions held at the Cathedral of Saint John the Divine in New York on October 7, 1984. He is a tiny person, deeply wrinkled, with two huge sacks under his eyes. No one could understand his broken English, but just to look at this man was sufficient to know what he stood for. The focus of the meeting was to raise the consciousness of the participants about the necessity of a commitment to peace as an essential aspect of religion in our time. Representatives of the World Religions were speaking as one voice and proclaiming that war in our time is indefensible. Since the monumental weaponry of our time inevitably destroys vast numbers of civilians, the only alternative nations can morally make use of in the defense of their territories and interests are nonviolent means of resistance. This stance underlines the necessity of supporting and strengthening international bodies of arbitration, the United Nations in particular.

Later there was a private meeting of leaders from the different world religions at the United Nations Church Center. Dom Helder was invited to speak about the situation of the poor in Brazil. It is a misnomer to call the people that he has served all his life "the poor." They are rather the destitute. Jesus said, "You will always have the poor with you." He did not say, "You will always have the destitute." The destitute are our responsibility. As Dom Helder started to speak about the poor, he choked up and could not continue. The bags under his eyes filled up like fountains and the tears ran down his wrinkled face. For five minutes he could not speak. His mouth twitched every now and then, and we hoped he might be able to continue. We waited in rapt attention for him to express what he was trying to say, but he could not. The memory of the destitute and the realization of their desperate plight left him with just one response: tears. Nothing has ever so convinced me of what it means to be destitute as his face at that moment.

As people begin to feel uneasiness with the mindset that treats other people as if they were of less value than themselves, and as they sense the enormity of the global problems of hunger, oppression, and peace, they ask the question, "What can I as a single individual do?" Others may put the same basic question in this way: "How can I contribute to peace and justice when I myself am under the influence of my selfish desires for more pleasures and more security symbols, and the fear of losing control of my life situation?" The same question might be put in a slightly different way. "Do I have to wait until I have been completely purified before I can begin to serve others or practice the corporal works of mercy?"

To this Jesus replies, "I was hungry and you gave me food, I was thirsty and you gave me drink. I was a stranger and you welcomed me" (Matt. 25:35). In the light of these words, the exercise of compassion does not sound like a big deal. It could mean giving someone a cup of water, a smile, or showing concern to someone suffering a loss. We do not have to wait until we can speak at the United Nations or go to Moscow for a summit conference. Somebody is in need right next door, in our family, at work, on the bus—everywhere we turn.

Jesus sent his disciples out two by two to work miracles and to preach the gospel before they were remotely prepared to do so; they were even less prepared to handle the success they achieved. When they arrived back from their journeys, they exultingly proclaimed, "The demons are subject to us in your name!" (Luke 10:20). They expected to be patted on the back. On the contrary, Jesus said, "Do not get excited about that kind of success. Anybody can work miracles with a little psychic energy and the divine assistance. What you should rejoice over is that your names are written in heaven." That is to say, "You have the destiny to enter the kingdom of God and to transmit the values of the kingdom to the people you love and to whom I am sending you."

The failure of our efforts to serve teaches us how to serve: that is, with complete dependence on divine inspiration. This is what changes the world.

24

Spirituality in Everyday Life

The primary spiritual practice is fidelity to one's commitments in daily life. The same old routines, failures, difficulties, and temptations keep recurring endlessly and seem to take us nowhere. The journey through the desert to which God subjected the Israelites mirrors our own spiritual journey through daily life.

It is difficult to perceive daily life in terms of the biblical desert unless we practice a form of non-conceptual prayer. A commitment to the contemplative dimension of the Gospel is the keystone to accepting the guidance of the Holy Spirit both in prayer and in action. The soil of our souls is like hardpan; it does not easily let go of the emotional weeds. We need the deepest kind of physical and mental rest in order to restore to our bodies their natural capacities to evacuate the harmful material that blocks the free flow of grace.

Centering prayer is addressed to the human situation just as it is. It is designed to heal the consequences of the human condition, which is basically the privation of the divine presence. Everyone suffers from this disease. If we accept the fact that we are suffering from a serious pathology, we possess a point of departure for the spiritual journey. The pathology is simply this: we have come to full reflective self-consciousness without the experience of intimacy with God.

Because that crucial reassurance is missing, our fragile egos desperately seek other means of shoring up our weaknesses and defending ourselves from the pain of alienation from God and other people. Contemplative prayer is the divine remedy for this illness.

Anthony of Egypt discovered and organized the four basic elements of the contemplative lifestyle: solitude, silence, simplicity, and a discipline for prayer and action. Monastic life is an environment designed to support the practice of these essential elements of spiritual health.

Contemplative prayer combines these four elements in a capsule that can be taken twice a day. The period of deep prayer, like a capsule, acts like an antibiotic to heal the psychotoxins of the human condition. There are ways in which we can work the effects of contemplative prayer into daily life and thus maximize the benefits of the prayer itself. Following are some suggestions as to how this might be done.

Dismantling the emotional programs

The disease of the human condition as we saw, is the false self, which, when sufficiently frustrated, is ready to trample on the rights and needs of others, as well as on our own true good, in order to ease its own pain or to obtain what it wants. By dismantling the emotional programs, we are working to heal the disease and not just the symptoms. The emotional programs were developed by repeated acts. With God's help, they can be taken down by repeated acts.

A good practice for daily life is the deliberate dismantling of our chief emotional program for happiness. By noticing the emotion that most often disturbs us and the particular event or memory that triggered the emotional upset, we can usually identify the program that is its source. If we then deliberately let go of the desire to avoid something or to have something, we have made a choice that undermines the habitual emotional reaction. This practice is not just a matter of lopping off dead branches, but also aims at changing the roots of the tree, which in this metaphor are our basic motivations. If we are bearing a grudge, we will continue to become angry at every provocation until we change the value system in the unconscious that is the source of the frustration which our anger is faithfully recording. All the resolution in the world not to get angry will not change anything until we deliberately address the source of the problem. When the root of the problem is healed, the afflictive emotions no longer go off in response to the frustration of our emotional programs for happiness, whether conscious or unconscious.

To summarize the practice once again: when you notice a particular upsetting emotion recurring frequently in daily life, name it without analyzing or reflecting on it. Then identify the event that triggered the emotion. In this way you can sleuth back to the emotional program that has been frustrated. Sometimes more than one program is involved at the same time. Then, say, "I give up my desire to control. . . I give up my desire for approval and affection . . . I let go of my desire for security. . ."

Obviously this practice is not going to dismantle the false self all at once, but by consistently letting go of our principal program for happiness, we begin to see how often it goes off and how much it influences our reactions, judgments, and behavior; as a result, we become more deeply motivated to let go of the emotion as soon as it arises.

It is important to let go of the emotion before it sets off our customary set of commentaries. Once our commentaries are activated, they reinforce the afflictive emotions, and once the emotional pot starts boiling, we may have a long wait for it to simmer down. The afflictive emotions release chemicals in the body, which may require the liver several hours to filter out.

If we have a duty to correct someone like a child or a friend, this is best done when our emotions are calm. Times when we are upset are not good times to correct a situation, unless the need to do something at once is very urgent. We only reinforce our habitual patterns by blasting our friends or shouting at the children.

Moving beyond group loyalty

Another practice is that of disengaging ourselves from over-identification with the cultural conditioning we received and toward which we feel deep loyalties or special ties. These dispositions are basically good in themselves, but as we move into interior freedom, God calls us to take personal responsibility for more and more of our decisions and actions. As we saw, the characteristics of the mental egoic consciousness are taking personal responsibility for our emotional life, no longer projecting our difficulties on others, and reappraising the parental or peer-group values that we accepted without question in early life.

The active prayer sentence

Another practice for daily life is to work an active prayer sentence of six to twelve syllables into our memory by saying it at moments when we are not engaged in a kind of activity that requires our attention. It can be a sentence from scripture or words of our own choice. The hesychastic practice of saying the "Jesus Prayer" in Orthodox Christianity is a model for this discipline. According to the teaching of *The Way of the Pilgrim*, when the "Jesus Prayer" has been repeated day after day for a long time, it enters the heart and starts to repeat itself. The Desert Fathers used to say verses from the psalms. Several of their favorites have been enshrined in the divine office: "Oh God, come to my assistance! Oh Lord, make haste to help me!" Or, "Our help is in the name of the Lord." It takes a lot of determination and time to work a sentence into our memory by saying it again and again, but these times will present themselves if we are alert to make use of them. Most people spend a couple of hours a day in more or less mindless activity—taking a shower, doing the dishes, driving a car, walking to work, waiting for a bus or for the phone to ring.

Once worked into the memory, this new "tape" tends to erase the prerecorded tapes already in place. Whenever one of the emotional programs is frustrated, a painful emotion promptly records the fact, and an appropriate commentary arises from our store of prerecorded tapes: "How can this happen to me?... How cruel everybody is to me! ... I'm no good." If we have worked a sentence into our subconscious memory that is about the same length as our normal commentaries, it erases the former tapes and thus reduces the force of the upsetting emotions. If there is no commentary, the process of building up emotional binges is less likely to take place. That gives us a neutral zone in which we can decide what to do.

The following story exemplifies the effects of the active prayer sentence. A certain woman was driving down a country road, hugging the center to avoid hitting a boy on a bicycle. A man drove up behind her, who was in a great hurry and wanted to pass her. He did not see the boy on the bicycle and did not understand why the woman was nudging the center of the road. He kept honking the horn, meaning, "Get out of the way!" When she did not move over to let him pass, his program of rage and accompanying commentaries took over. Pushing the accelerator to the floor, he zoomed around her and, as he passed, rolled down the window, shouted obscene words at her, and spat right in her face! Anger, shame, hurt feelings, and grief all started to surface in the woman. At the same time, her store of commentaries also began to arise: "How could someone be so cruel? How could God allow this to happen? . . . All men are beasts!"

Just as she was about to lose control, up came her active prayer sentence: "How sweet and pleasant it is for people to live together in unity!" The new tape erased the old tapes, and she entered into a neutral zone where she was not preprogrammed to react one way or the other. Into that empty space rushed the Holy Spirit saying, "Love the guy!" A wave of peace flooded her whole being. She was filled with love, joy, and all the other fruits of the Spirit. She forgave the man from the bottom of her heart and drove on down the road as if she had just received a bouquet of roses.

This example points in a special way to the practical purpose that all the various means of bringing the effects of contemplative prayer into everyday life actually serve. They cultivate a neutral zone or open space within us from which we can *decide* what to do. That is true freedom. The neutral zone enables God, according to circumstances, to manifest all the fruits of the Spirit in and through us: charity, joy, peace, patience, gentleness, goodness, self-control, and meekness.

Self-acceptance

Another practice for daily life is to cultivate the loving acceptance of ourselves. Encounter groups made a great contribution in the sixties and seventies by teaching people who had never really experienced their feelings to begin to do so. If certain levels of our being have been damaged in early life, a program such as the encounter groups provide can be helpful. The mistake would be to glorify the program as if it were able to heal every problem. In the sixties and seventies, encounter groups opened people to feelings that had previously been repressed for ethnic, cultural, or other reasons. People found the liberating of their emotions from repression so wonderful that they almost made a religion out of process. A program designed to heal one level of consciousness cannot heal every other level all by itself. Other levels need their special remedies too.

Compassion for ourselves is an important disposition because all our emotional programs are fully in place by the time we are four or five, certainly by the age of seven or eight, and hence are not our fault. The more we were damaged as children by inconsiderate treatment, the greater our compensatory needs and the more firmly our emotional programs are likely to be in place. For instance, there is an 80 percent chance that physically abused children will, in turn, abuse their own children. Child battering is the chief cause of death of children under seven in this country. Without deep therapy, those who were abused perpetuate the same horrors on their children that they endured. Those with repressed rage may find in an infant the first helpless person on whom that rage can be expressed. The tendency seems to be strong to repeat what was done to us—to project our own problems on someone else and then to offer that helpless person as a victim sacrifice to satisfy our rage.

When we suffer some great loss or feel that our conduct has damaged our children or experience an important relationship breaking apart, we may find ourselves overwhelmed with guilt feelings. This is the time to say, "I accept it all. I will try with God's help to learn from this experience." When there is no way to correct the damage, as is often the case, we have to turn it over to God and ask him to reduce the consequences. Then we can work to dismantle the emotional programs that were the cause of the tragedy. That is the best contribution we can make to righting the wrongs that may have occurred in our lives. When we try to bring about change in ourselves, we are guaranteeing that it will not happen again. And it is the only guarantee we can have.

Sometimes we need to sit with feelings instead of trying to get away from them. We may be experiencing guilt, loneliness, or the boredom that goes with loneliness. If we sit with painful emotions, name them, feel them, and accept them, saying, "Yes, I feel guilt. . . anger. . . panic; I accept them, I embrace them," then we can stare down our feelings. What we are embracing in these painful emotions is not the suffering itself, but the God of love who dwells somehow at the bottom of them. In this way, grace is released and begins to reduce the pain. To sit with our suffering is one of the fastest ways to work through it. We may need a friend to confide in, and, in certain cases, medication or psychotherapy. Every kind of help can be pressed into service, but the radical healing is the acceptance of the situation, because in some way God is present there.

God always offers a way out. If we sit still, we are more likely to see what it is. If we act out our feelings to get away from the pain, we end up back where we started. Around and around we go. Human misery keeps evil alive. As soon as we accept the situation and forgive the people involved, the devil drops dead. The devil and his influence can exist and thrive only on our refusal to love and our unwillingness to forgive.

Guard of the heart

Another practice to bring the effects of contemplative prayer into daily life is traditionally known as "guard of the heart." This consists of letting go of every emotional disturbance as soon as it arises and before we start to think about it. This is a more sophisticated method than dismantling the emotional programs for happiness because it deals with the whole of life. Guard of the heart is based on the sense of interior peace that comes when our wills are united by intention with God's will. Whenever that basic sense of peace is disturbed, we reaffirm our intention to be united with God's will by some simple but appropriate act. The attentiveness to abide in this union of wills might be compared to a radio beam that guides an airplane. If the plane moves off course, the signal changes, warning the pilot to readjust his direction.

Following are three ways of keeping ourselves on course in everyday affairs: the first is to cast disturbing thoughts as soon as they arise into the lap of God, or to give them to Jesus as a gift. The second is to give our entire attention to whatever we are doing when we notice disturbing thoughts; we concentrate on the activity of the moment and refuse to think of them. Finally, if we find ourselves unoccupied when disturbing thoughts arise, we may grab a book or take up some prearranged project and thus avoid thinking about the upsetting situation and setting off the commentaries that initiate or reinforce interior turmoil.

Lectio divina

Another practice for daily life is *lectio divina,* listening to the word of God in scripture as a means of deepening our relationship with him on the levels of reflection and spontaneous prayer. Daily *lectio divina* is especially important since it leads to the contemplative practice of resting in God and provides an ongoing conceptual background for it. In fact, contemplative prayer was traditionally seen by the Fathers of the Church as the final stage of *lectio divina,* the natural result of reading and reflecting on the word of God with a listening heart. Other forms of spiritual reading also contribute to our knowledge and motivation to sustain the journey.

In addition many find it helpful to keep "minute books." They write down a few sentences from scripture that they like or find helpful.

While waiting for the phone or bus, instead of doing nothing or look-ing around to no purpose, they take their "minute books" from their purses or pockets and read a few lines. It is astonishing how quickly our best resolutions are forgotten. We need to propagandize our-selves throughout the day—to give ourselves short commercials, so to speak—to remind ourselves of what we really want to do.

Joining a support group

A weekly support group that practices some form of contemplative prayer has the advantage of pooling silence, which is a kind of lit-urgy, as well as providing encouragement to each other. Such a group helps to renew our resolution to persevere in prayer if we have slipped for a good or not-so-good reason. Sharing prayer together, especially silent prayer, increases faith. In addition, if it is customary in our tra-dition, we should participate in a worshiping community and receive the Eucharist.

Conclusion

What is described here is not just a smorgasbord of practices intended to bring the effects of centering prayer into daily life; nor is it just a method of prayer and a conceptual background to motivate us to persevere in it. What is being proposed in this book and in the other two books of the trilogy, *Open Mind, Open Heart,* and *The Mystery of Christ,* is a commitment to the contemplative dimension of the gospel. This commitment addresses the whole of our being and all our activity, whatever our states of life may be. A total surrender of ourselves to the spiritual journey is required, not just a patchwork of exercises that are part of daily life but do not affect the whole of it or penetrate the various aspects of our lives. When we begin the spiritual journey in earnest with a program of centering prayer as a path to contemplation, we are initiating a dynamic that involves our personal responses to Christ and affects our whole lives. These practices, along with our prayer, are a holistic response to Christ's invitation, "Come follow me."

The commitment of lay people and those in active ministries to contemplation is a new way of following Christ in our time. Just as the Spirit created a new way of following Christ at the close of the age of martyrdom by inspiring Anthony with his vision of the monastic lifestyle, so now the Holy Spirit is inviting lay persons and those in active ministries to become contemplatives where they are, to move beyond the restricted world of selfishness into service of their communities, and to join all others of goodwill in addressing the global problems of our time: poverty, hunger, oppression, violence, and above all, the refusal to love.

Appendix I
(See Chapters 1–3)

The False Self In Action

WAYS OF REACTING TO FRUSTRATIONS OF EMOTIONAL CENTERS	WAYS OF REACTING ACCORDING TO TEMPERAMENT	WAYS OF EXPRESSING ONE'S EMOTIONAL PROGRAMMING
Grief (refusal to let go of loved possession) Self-pity Discouragement	**Withdrawal** Tendency to passivity and to swallow the hurt	**Materialistic** Workaholism Possessiveness Wealth, money, property Luxurious food and drink Sports
Apathy (withdrawal from life) Boredom Bitterness Aversion for others Sloth Despair	**Aggression** Tendency to fight back **Dependency** Tendency to rely on strong figure in environment	**Emotional** People pleasing Satisfying relationships Emotional exchange Sexual misconduct Certain kinds of music
Lust (greed) Overweening desire for bodily, mental, or spiritual satisfactions Compulsive acting out		**Intellectual** Academic excellence Need to be always right
Pride Overweening desire for fame, wealth, or power Desire for vindictive triumph Vanity Self-hatred in face of failure		**Social** Status Prestige Racism Nationalism Forms of domination Authoritarianism
Anger Hostility Desire for revenge		**Religious** Legalism Pharisaism Hypocrisy Prejudice/bigotry Cults
Envy/Jealousy (sadness at another's good) Competitiveness Loneliness		**Spiritual** Attachment to psychic powers Attachment to spiritual consolation

Appendix II

(See Chapters 4–6)

The Human Condition

LEVELS OF CONSCIOUSNESS	CULTURAL EVOLUTION	INDIVIDUAL EVOLUTION
Mental Egoic* (Zeus, symbol of reason, slaying the dragon, symbol of primitive instinct and emotion)	3000 B.C.E. to present	8 years to adulthood
Mythic Membership (King as embodiment of city state or nation)	12,000 B.C.E.	4 to 8 years old
Typhonic (half-human, half-animal)	200,000 B.C.E.	2 to 4 years old
Reptilian (serpent eating its tail)	5 million years B.C.E.	0 to 2 years old

* Emergence of mental egoic powers prepares way for higher levels of consciousness (sec p. 142). But unless the emotional programs for happiness arc directly confronted, reason is co-opted to rationalize, justify, and glorify the values they represent.

SOCIETAL CHARACTERISTICS	PRIMARY DEVELOPMENTAL CHARACTERISTICS
Industrial/technological society Participational government	Full reflective self-consciousness Emergence of reason Personal responsibility
Stratification of society Verbalization Socialization Farming society Authoritarian government Wars	Overidentification with group affiliation Conformity to group Values Fear of death Full formation of false self
Magical Hunting society Living from day to day	Formation of body-self Formation of power/control center Formation of affection/esteem center
Immersed in nature	No consciousness' of a self Dependence on mother Prompt fulfillment of instinctual needs Formation of security/survival center

Appendix III

(See Chapters 8–22)

Comparison of Christian Spiritual Journey and Evolutionary Model

EVOLUTIONARY MODE (Chain of being)	CHRISTIAN SPIRITUAL JOURNEY
Levels of Consciousness	**Levels of Relating to God**
7. Unity	Unity (wisdom)
6. Unitive	Transforming Union (holiness) Night of Spirit
5. Intuitive	Stages of Prayer (Teresa of Avila) prayer of full union prayer of union prayer of quiet infused recollection Night of Sense
4. Mental Egoic (full reflective self-consciousness)	*Lectio Divina* contemplative prayer affective prayer discursive meditation reading of scripture
3. Mythic Membership (group overidentification	
2. Typhonic	
1. Reptilian	

Notes

Chapter Four: The Human Condition

1 Ken Wilber, *Up From Eden* (Boulder, Colo.: Shambhala Publications, 1983).
2 See, for example, Ernest Becker, *The Denial of Death* (New York: Free Press, 1973) and Norman O. Brown, *Life Against Death* (Middletown, Conn.: Wesleyan Univ. Press, 1959).

Chapter Seven: Mental Egoic Consciousness

1 P. Campbell and E. McMahon, *Bio-Spirituality* (Chicago: Loyola Univ. Press, 1985), ch. 6.

Chapter Eight: The Four Consents

1 John S. Dunne, *Time and Myth* (Garden City, N.Y.: Doubleday, 1973).

Chapter Ten: Anthony as a Paradigm of the Spiritual Journey

1 Athanasius, *The Life of Saint Anthony,* trans. Robert T. Meyer (Westminster: Newman Press, 1950).

Chapter Twelve: Special Trials in the Night of Sense

1 Saint John of the Cross, *Dark Night of the Soul,* trans, and ed. E. Allison Peers (Garden City, N.Y.: Image Books, 1959), bk. I, ch. XIV, no. 1.

Chapter Thirteen: Anthony in the Tombs

1 Athanasius, *The Life of Saint Anthony,* trans. Robert T. Meyer (Westminster: Newman Press, 1950).

2 In Christopher Isherwood, ed., *Vedanta and the Western World* (London: George Allen & Unwin, 1961).

Chapter Twenty One: A Pure Faith

1 Ruth Burrows, *Guidelines for Mystical Prayer* (Denville, N.J.: Dimension Books, 1980).

Glossary of Terms

Afflictive Emotions — chiefly anger, fear, and discouragement, which are the spontaneous feeling reactions to the failure to acquire things perceived to be good and difficult to attain, or to the failure to avoid things perceived to be evil and difficult to avoid. Afflictive emotions include the capital sins enumerated by Evagrius, The Desert Father of the fourth century, which are a combination of several emotions: pride, vanity, envy, gluttony, greed, lust, anger, and apathy.

Centering Prayer — a contemporary form of prayer of the heart, prayer of simplicity, or prayer of faith; a method of reducing obstacles to the gift of contemplative prayer and of developing habits conducive to responding to the inspirations of the Spirit.

Consent — an act of the will expressing acceptance of someone, something, or some course of action; the manifestation of one's intention.

Consolations — among spiritual writers, this term generally refers to the sensible pleasure derived from devotional practices such as *lectio divina*, discursive meditation, prayer, liturgy, and good works. Such consolations may arise from sensible stimuli, imagination, memory, and reflection, or from purely spiritual sources such as the fruits of the spirit and the beatitudes.

Contemplation	a synonym for contemplative prayer.
Contemplative Living	activity in daily life prompted by the gifts of the Spirit; the fruit of a contemplative attitude.
Contemplative Prayer	the development of one's relationship with Christ to the point of communing beyond words, thoughts, and feelings; a process moving from the simplified activity of waiting upon God to the ever-increasing predominance of the gifts of the Spirit as the source of one's prayer.
Divine Therapy	a paradigm in which the spiritual journey is presented as a form of psychotherapy designed to heal the emotional wounds of early childhood and our mechanisms for coping with them.
Divine Union	a term describing either a single experience of the union of all the faculties in God, or the permanent state of union called transforming union (see transforming union).
Ecstasy	the temporary suspension by the divine action of the thinking and feeling faculties, including at times the external senses, which facilitates the experience of the prayer of full union.
Emotional Programs for Happiness	the growth of the instinctual needs of survival/ security, affection/esteem, and power/control into centers of motivation, around which our thoughts, feelings, and behavior gravitate.
False Self	the self developed in our own likeness rather than in the likeness of God; the self-image developed to cope with the emotional trauma of early childhood. It seeks happiness in satisfying the instinctual needs of survival/security, affection /esteem, and power/control, and bases its self-worth on cultural or group identification.

Human Condition	a way of describing the consequences of original sin which are: illusion (not knowing how to find the happiness for which we are inherently programmed); concupiscence (the pursuit of happiness where it cannot be found); weakness of will (the inability to pursue happiness where it is to be found, unaided by grace).
Intuitive Consciousness	the level of consciousness beyond rational thinking (not to be identified with bodily intuition), characterized by harmony, cooperation, forgiveness, negotiation to resolve differences, mutuality rather than competitiveness; a sense of oneness with others and of belonging to the universe.
Mental Egoic Consciousness	the development of full reflective self-consciousness, beginning with the capacity for logical reasoning at about eight years of age and arriving at abstract thinking around twelve or thirteen; characterized by the sense of personal responsibility and guilt feelings regarding one's attitudes and behavior.
Mystical Prayer	in the terminology of this book, a synonym for contemplative prayer.
Mythic Membership Consciousness	the unquestioned assimilation of the values and ideas of one's social group; overidentification with one's family, ethnic, or religious community from which one draws one's identity and self-worth, and conformity to the group's value systems. It is characterized socially by the stratification of society into hierarchical forms.
Original Sin	a way of explaining the universal experience of coming to full reflective self-consciousness without the inner conviction or experience of union with God.

Purification	an essential part of the process of contemplation through which the dark side of one's personality, mixed motivation, and the emotional pain of a lifetime, stored in the unconscious, are gradually evacuated; the necessary preparation for transforming union.
Reptilian Consciousness	the level of consciousness characterized by immersion in nature, prompt fulfillment of instinctual needs, and no consciousness of a self.
Spirituality	a life of faith in interior submission to God and pervading all one's motivation and behavior; a life of prayer and action prompted by the inspirations of the Holy Spirit; a disposition not limited to devotional practices, rituals, liturgy, or other particular acts of piety or service to others, but rather the catalyst that integrates, unifies, and directs all one's activity.
Spiritual Attentiveness	the general loving attention to the presence of God in pure faith, characterized either by an undifferentiated sense of unity or by a more personal attention to one or other of the Divine Persons.
Spiritual Senses	a teaching common among the Fathers of the Church to describe the stages of contemplative prayer through the analogy of the external senses of smell, touch, and taste. The point of the comparison is the immediacy of the experience.
Transformation (Transforming Union)	the stable sharing by all dimensions of the human person in God's life and loving presence, rather than a particular experience or set of experiences; a restructuring of consciousness in which the divine reality is perceived to be present in oneself and in all that is.

True Self — the image of God in which every human being is created; our participation in the divine life manifested in our uniqueness.

Typhonic Consciousness — the level of consciousness characterized by development of a body-self distinct from other objects. It is characterized by the inability to distinguish the part from the whole, and images in the imagination from external reality.

Ultimate Mystery/ Ultimate Reality — the ground of infinite potentiality and actualization; a term emphasizing the divine transcendence.

Unitive Consciousness — the experience of transforming union together with the process of working the experience of divine love into all one's faculties and relationships.

Unloading the Unconscious — the spontaneous release of previously unconscious emotional material from early childhood in the form of primitive feelings or a barrage of images or commentaries; it may occur both during the time of contemplative prayer and outside the time of prayer.

Bibliography

Bouyer, Louis. *A History of Christian Spirituality*, 3 vols. New York: Seabury Press, 1982.

Butler, Cuthbert. *Western Mysticism,* New York: Dutton, 1923.

Dupre, Louis, and James A. Wiseman, eds. *Light from Light: An Anthology of Christian Mysticism*. Mahwah, N.J.: Paulist Press, 1988.

Lossky, Vladimir. *The Mystical Theology of the Eastern Church*. London: J. Clarke, 1957.

McGinn, Bernard, ed. *The Presence of God: A History of Western Civilization Mysticism*. Vol. 1, *The Foundations of Western Mysticism*. New York: Crossroad, 1991.

Merton, Thomas. *The Wisdom of the Desert*. New York: New Directions, 1970.

Thompson, William N. *Jesus: Lord and Savior*. Mahwah, N.J.: Paulist Press, 1980.

Ware, Timothy. *The Art of Prayer: An Orthodox Anthology*. Salem, N.H.: Faber & Faber, 1966.

Selected Classic Sources of the Christian Contemplative Tradition

Bernard of Clairvaux. *Selected Works*. Classics of Western Spirituality Series. Mahwah, N.J.: Paulist Press, 1987.

Cassian, John. *Conferences*. In *Western Asceticism*. Translated by Owen Chadwick. Philadelphia: Westminster Press, 1958.

Evagrius Pontious. *The Praktikos: Chapters on Prayer*. Translated by John Eudes Bamberger. Spencer, Mass. Cistercian Publications, 1970.

Gregg, Robert, ed. *Athanasius: Life of Anthony*. Classics of Western Spirituality Series. Mahwah, N.J.: Paulist Press, 1988.

Gregory of Nyssa. *The Life of Moses*. Classics of Western Spirituality Series. Mahwah, N.J. Paulist Press, 1978.

———. *Commentary on the Song of Songs*. Translated by Casimir McCambley. Brookline, Mass.: Hellenic College Press, 1987.

Johnson, William, ed. *The Cloud of Unknowing*. New York: Doubleday, Image Books, 1973.

Kavanaugh, Kieran, and Otilio Rodriguez, trans. *The Collected Works of John of the Cross*. Washington, D.C.: ICS Publications, 1979.

Lawrence of the Resurrection. *The Practice of the Presence of God*. Springfield, Ill.: Templegate Press, 1974.

Maximus the Confessor. *Selected Writings*. Classics of Western Spirituality Series. Mahwah, N.J.: Paulist Press, 1985.

Meister Eckhart. *Sermons and Treatises.* 3 vols. Translated and edited by M. O'C. Walshe. Shaftesbury, UK: Element Books, 1987.

Pseudo-Dionysius. *The Complete Works.* Classics of Western Spirituality Series. Mahwah, N.J.: Paulist Press, 1987.

Ruusbroac, John. *The Spiritual Espousals and Other Works.* Classics of Western Spirituality Series. Mahwah, N.J.: Paulist Press, 1985.

Teresa of Avila. *The Interior Castle.* Classics of Western Spirituality Series. Mahwah, N.J.: Paulist Press, 1979.

Thérèse of Lisieux. *The Story of a Soul.* Translated by John Clarke. Washington, D.C.: ICS Publications, 1976.

William of St. Thierry. *Commentary on the Song of Songs.* Kalamazoo, Mich.: Cistercian Publications, 1969.

Selected Contemporary Expressions of the Christian Contemplative Tradition

Burrows, Ruth. *Guidelines for Mystical Prayer.* Denville, N.J.: Dimension Books, 1980.

Green, William. *When the Well Runs Dry.* Notre Dame, Ind.: Ave Maria Press, 1985.

Hall, Thelma. *Too Deep For Words.* Mahwah, N.J.: Paulist Press, 1989.

Johnston, William. *The Mysticism of the Cloud of Unknowing.* Trabuco Canyon, Calif: Source Books, 1987.

Keating, Thomas. *Open Mind, Open Heart.* Rockport, Mass.: Element Books, 1986.

———. *The Mystery of Christ.* Rockport, Mass.: Element Books, 1991.

Maloney, George A. *Prayer of the Heart.* Notre Dame, Ind.: Ave Maria Press, 1981.

Merton, Thomas. *New Seeds of Contemplation.* New York: New Directions, 1972.

———. *Contemplative Prayer.* New York: Doubleday, Image Books, 1971.

Nemeck, Francis K. and Marie T. Coombs. *Contemplation.* Wilmington, Del.: Michael Glazier, 1984.

Pennington, Basil. *Centering Prayer.* New York: Doubleday, Image Books, 1980.

The Psychology of the Spiritual Journey

Assagioli, Robert. *Psychosynthesis,* New York: Penguin Books, 1965.

Bradshaw, John. *Bradshaw on: The Family.* Deerfield Beach, Fla.: Health Communications, 1988.

Campbell, Peter and Edwin McMahon. *Bio-Spirituality.* Chicago: Loyola University Press, 1983.

Keyes, Ken, Jr., and Penny Keyes. *Handbook to Higher Consciousness.* Berkeley, Calif.: Line Books, 1975.

May, Gerald. *Will and Spirit.* New York: Harper & Row, 1983.

———. *Addiction and Grace.* San Francisco: Harper & Row, 1988.

Schaef, Anne Wilson. *When Society Becomes an Addict.* San Francisco: Harper & Row, 1987.

———. *Co-Dependency.* San Francisco: Harper & Row, 1986.

Wilber, Ken. *Up from Eden.* Boulder, Colo.: Shambhala, 1981.

———. *No Boundary.* Boulder, Colo.: Shambhala, 1979.

Washburn, Michael. *The Ego and the Dynamic Ground.* Albany, New York: State University of New York Press, 1988.

Contemplative Outreach is an international spiritual network of individuals and small faith communities committed to renewing the contemplative dimension of the Gospel in everyday life. Contemplative Outreach, Ltd. welcomes the opportunity to serve by offering:

♦ Networking Assistance
♦ Establishment of Local Centering Prayer Programs
♦ On-going Centering Prayer Groups
♦ Books, Video and Audio Recordings, and digital downloads
♦ Centering Prayer Retreats
♦ Newsletters—Brochures

Please visit our website at:
www.contemplativeoutreach.org

or contact us at:

Contemplative Outreach Ltd.
10 Park Place—2nd Floor—Suite 2B
Butler, NJ 07405
Phone: 973-838-3384
Fax: 973-492-5795
E-mail: office@coutreach.org